Jean-Claude l

Total Horsem

Jean-Claude Racinet

TOTAL
HORSEMANSIP

XENOPHON PRESS

Published by Xenophon Press, 1772 Middlehurst Road, Cleveland Heights, Ohio 44118-1648, U.S.A.

ISBN 0-933316-13-5

This book is dedicated to the memory of Commandant Gérard de Pommier, mounted cavalry officer and officer of the French Foreign Legion.

Foreword

This book is not a riding manual. It will not teach you how to pass a flying lead change, how to piaffe or how to passage. Besides, no book can teach you those things; but some books can lead you to the path, by giving you exercises, proceedings and even "tricks" which will help you in your groping endeavor. Yet their value, however certain, is limited, because they don't know how you ride, what is your stiffness (or suppleness), what is your personality (if you are tense, your horse will be tense, if you are irresolute, your horse will be irresolute, etc.).They don't know the softness, or warmth, or sensuousness, or rudeness of your hands. Nor do they know your horse's problems and your horse's personality.

So horsemanship is a solitary discovery.

Eight years ago I wrote the manual **Another Horsemanship** which was published by Xenophon Press. This time, I would like to consider the matter from a more elevated view point, and content myself with giving the reader the absolute recipe for absolute balance, wherefrom all proceeds.

So this book is a Gospel, this latter word meaning, as you know, "good news." But like any Gospel, its efficiency will depend on the quality of "penetration" of the reader's mind. Its message will be received inasmuch as the reader will be wanting for it. To grow and blossom, the seed has to fall on the propitious terrain.

Preface

To give a book a title is not an easy task. It should sum up the book's meaning from the author's point of view, but it should also attract the reader, for who ever wrote a book and didn't care about its being read? And sometimes those two concerns may clash.

When I titled one of my books **Another Horsemanship**, for instance, I did it with the reader's point of view in mind. I knew that due to the rapid development of dressage in the USA, due to the omnipresence of the Germans in all the compartments of this discipline, from breeding to judging to competing to selling, chances were that most American riders would have been confronted with only one type of horsemanship. This horsemanship wasn't mine, so I decided to herald my message as "another" horsemanship. Yet had I yielded to my deep inclination, I would have titled it "Horsemanship," or "True Horsemanship," or "The True Classical Horsemanship," etc. But I knew that for the lay reader, I was a man out of the mainstream, and it would have been foolish to ignore it.

Years later, it dawned on me that I had been more "trendy" than I thought, since "alternative" medicine is a vocable and a reality more and more acknowledged, and I was offering an alternative. As in the case of "riding in lightness," alternative medicines sometimes are just good medicines of yesterday that have fallen into oblivion or been obliterated by powerful interests. As, for instance, homeopathy. Or, for that matter, osteopathy.

Now, I titled the present book **Total Horsemanship** because that is exactly what it is about, but I must say that "Holistic Horsemanship" was very tempting as well. What I like in holistic medicine is not so much that it considers the organism as a whole but the fact that it endeavors to treat the causes and not the effects. Classical medicine too often thinks that by suppressing the effects, one will give the cause its leave. And I can agree with that when there is no other way, though I am not sure the cause is not lying dormant somewhere.

Like modern medicine, modern equitation offers some great - and expensive - achievements, but it leaves many unsatisfied, because it takes the problems from outside and not from inside, from the symptoms more than from the imbalances which foster disease. What attracts me in Baucherism is that it tries to take the riding problem from inside, and exactly as an acupuncturist will endeavor to restore the balance of the flow of energy in the diverse meridians and then let the body heal itself, Baucher will work on balance first, and then let the horse do.

But I also suspected that something had eluded Baucher, that, in his search for the causes of imbalance, he had not gone as far as he would have liked. I understood that there were sometimes limitations in the results; without calling into question the principle of the method, they were nagging, and opposed to the very ideal of Baucher himself, who wanted to find a theory evenly applicable to all horses.

And then I discovered Giniaux, and with him, the "missing link" (that could also have been a title for this book). Giniaux's equine osteopathy allowed me to explain the occasional limitations of Baucher, and in the meantime to vindicate him.

So much so that if you asked me to give you the three greatest names in the history of horsemanship, I would say, "La Guérinière, Baucher, and Giniaux."

You see, I am a very modest man.

But by the way, who am I to pretend to give lessons to others?

Because of my age and the fact that I spent over seventeen years in the French Army as an officer in the prime of my life, my students sometimes conjure up a past of glorious cavalry charges, of frequentation with the most prestigious Riding Masters, of initiation to the real Art of Riding in some now defunct dream Academy. I would have loved for this to be true, but on the other hand, had this been "for real," I probably would not know what I know now.

My father fought four years in the trenches of World War One. In August 1914, as his Regiment entered Belgium to establish contact with the enemy, the Colonel was told by scouts that the Germans were close by. Then the Colonel went ahead on horseback to see for himself. Moments later, his body was found riddled with thirty-six bullets; it so happened that the Germans were armed with this ridiculous new invention called a machine gun. This was the end of the Cavalry.

The last Cavalry charge, as concerns the French Army, was waged one month later, in the plain of Senlis, thirty-five miles east of Paris. I was minus fifteen years of age.

Yet all my life, or almost, has been rolled by the rhythm of horses' hooves. I remember vividly the three Percherons my uncle in Normandy was so proud of, "Bayard," "Pâquerette," and "Junon." During the occupation, the Germans, who were pilfering our poor country, did not confiscate them, because of their grey coat, which made them easy to spot from an aircraft.

My first Master was a former "sous-maître de Manège" of the "Cadre Noir." He had been riding instructor at the Artillery School in Fontainebleau. He was an explosive mixture of radical feelings and tradition. As a former NCO at a time when social segregation was a fact of life in the cavalry, he was full of bitterness against the "old whigs" who, he thought, and probably rightfully so, had prevented him from expressing to the full his equestrian talent, and he was ready to adhere to any modernity, any novelty. Years later, in 1968, a time of great turmoil in France, when a pseudo Revolution had in fact chased the French government away (de Gaulle had fled for one day to Germany), and as I was already myself retired from the Army, Pizon came to see me and proposed to me to take the lead of a bunch of youngsters and...storm the offices of the French Equestrian Federation in Paris!

But he had been molded in the right crucible. He had this extraordinary deep and supple seat, acquired the hard way, that was the pride of the School of Saumur and always characterized the French School. In 1936, he had been chosen to ride the horses selected for the Olympic Games in Berlin, under the expert supervision of three colonels sitting on chairs in the middle of the "Manège": Colonel (future General) Decarpentry, Colonel Danloux (then "Ecuyer en Chef"), and Colonel Aublet. One can imagine worse sponsorship! Speaking of General Decarpentry, Pizon would forget the "General" and call him "Decarpentry," as if he had been a pal. They must now have interesting riding exchanges in the riders' paradise.

Coming back from Korea with two war injuries and a citation in 1953, I was lucky enough to be accepted in the "special riding course" of the Cavalry School. My instructor there was the late, lamented Colonel de Saint André, future "Ecuyer en Chef," then a Major. He was a wonderfully well organized brain, and a terrific teacher to boot. There was no aspect of the French Equestrian Tradition he did not know and could not comment on.

And then I was left on my own, but I rode quite a lot, since there were still a few horses in the French Army, for sport purpose in general, although I was once assigned for two months to a mounted Regiment of "Spahis" in Tunisia. I rode in Tunisia, then in Algeria until it became too difficult for reasons of political turmoil. I rode at the "Ecole Militaire" in Paris, where I had the honor to be chosen as a member of their jumping team.

In between, I had been involved with experiences of "counter-revolutionary warfare," another of my "hobby horses"; they had been successful and exhilarating, but they ran across the "wind of history," so in 1965 I retired as a captain.

And set out to make a living out of my riding expertise, which shows the extent of my naivety.

This was thirty-four years ago. Since that time, what have I done? I'm going to tell you: I have studied, and studied, and studied, and studied. I considered all my horses, good or less good, as an occasion for study. I specialized in "difficult" horses (I even ran ads) for this reason. I was on a quest for total collection for all horses, and as a prerequisite to boot. I knew it was possible, because if it was possible with some, it should be possible for all. There remained only to find out why there were discrepancies.

As time passed, I felt closer and closer to my goal, but still naggingly far away from it. A little as if you are climbing Mount Everest, and you see the summit, it's there, but you seem unable to reach it in reality. Four years ago, a young Andalusian stallion I was in charge of "breaking in" broke my leg. I didn't break him; he broke me. As I was lying down on a sofa, waiting for days for the swelling to subside and allow for a cast to be placed, I was impatient to heal, because I had devised new flexions which, I was sure, would definitely take care of the problem. But they didn't.

And then I understood that the last fifteen percent in the elevation of the withers that I could not get were due to vertebral blockings. And that was it.

I have always been interested in dressage, not as this sad and standoffish discipline that pretends to be exclusive from all the others, but as a technique applicable to all disciplines, and as an art. First, because horses are awkward animals, at least under the saddle. That's the technical aspect of the matter. Second, because it is a lot of fun making then dance. This is the Art.

I have reported at length in **Racinet explains Baucher** (Xenophon Press) and briefly in this book how I discovered Baucher. I discovered the advantages of the flexion of the jaw when I was a jumping rider, because balance is essential in jumping. No balance, no clear round. And the jaw flexion is a marvelous tool for balance. Besides, balance is everywhere in equitation. I once rode in a flat race; it is a lot of fun, and it gives one feelings of harmony and balance akin to those felt in dressage. Horsemanship is "one." I even wonder if the flexion of the jaw could not help the gallopers as well.

Dr. Giniaux, the world renowned equine osteopath without whom this book would never have been born, was apprised by myself of the flexion of the jaw. He introduced it in his manipulations and told me that racehorse trainers would ask him, after he had worked their horses in that fashion, "What did you do to my horse? Now, he pushes!"

Baucherism helping the racehorses. Enough to make Comte d'Aure shiver in his grave!

So I discovered Baucher and his flexions. Years later, I discovered Dr. Giniaux and his osteopathic manipulations. Now it so happens that the osteopathic manipulations are based on flexions, of the neck but of the body as well, and it so happens that, as I found out, the flexions of Baucher may constitute osteopathic manipulations. Here was the "missing link," and I set out to try a synthesis between the two disciplines, Baucherism and osteopathy. And found out that it was absolutely feasible.

I then started, not to manipulate, but to "flex" a little differently sometimes and a little farther than Baucher, and I coined the expression "flexion-relaxation," which describes as well as possible this new technique.

So now, I hope, we can practice a "total horsemanship." Please read and enjoy.

J. c Racinet

Contents

PART ONE

THE THESIS

Slanting the pelvis

In 1973, the French Equestrian Federation appointed Jean d'Orgeix as coach of France's International Jumping Team. He was given an office in the National School of Equitation at Saumur (an offspring of the Army Cavalry School), plus the use of all the installations necessary to carry out his mission, and he set out immediately to instruct a bunch of youngsters with no previous experience in International competition. He wanted to demonstrate that with his methods, he could rapidly train horses and riders to a high level. And so he did. In no time, his students figured convincingly at the International level.

One of d'Orgeix's contentions was that there were no reasons for buying highly expensive horses endowed with outstanding physical capabilities; all rested in the training. And apparently he made his point, since the horses his teenagers were performing with seemed to be coming out of nowhere.

But I observed that they all presented a common characteristic: they would briskly and thoroughly "tuck in" their pelvis by the slightest intervention of their riders' hands.

For years, I had been of the opinion that collection doesn't lie in the shortening of the horse's base of support, but in the shortening of his "middle line," that which joins the point of shoulders to the point of buttocks, entailing an elevation of the withers and a "tipping under" of the croup. And I could see my conviction justified by d'Orgeix's choice of horses.

A few years later, I attended the "Carrousel" at Saumur. The "Carrousel" is a celebration which takes place every year at the end of the studies of the cadets. Although the Army does not use horses for military purposes anymore, equitation as a sport remains mandatory for the cadets. At the "Carrousel" they present all those equestrian games which the old tradition has bequeathed to us, like poking a spear in a ring suspended in the air, chopping dummy heads with the sword from horseback, etc.

Some of these games require the rider to go full speed, then decelerate in a few strides and make a U-turn, a little like in a "passade." Now I observed that all those horses, who were not particularly athletic, would tuck their rear end in briskly and strongly when it came time to decelerate and turn on the haunches, after they had "darted." Of course, this did not surprise me, but what was interesting was the vivacity with which this tucking in gesture was done.

Still later in time, I came to the United States, where I was introduced to the Quarterhorse. Quarterhorses have a marvelous balance, which is the reason why they are used to "work" the cattle, a task which requires much mobility. Now this balance may be surprising for a European, because by European standards, Quarterhorses are ill built: too long in their back, too short in their front legs.

What saves them, however, is the way they use their marvelously powerful rear end; at a trot, for instance, their hind hooves set down way ahead of the vertical projection of the stifle, and do not back much farther than the vertical projection of their point of buttocks. Meaning that this rear end works beneath the mass, because their pelvis remains naturally, effortlessly "tucked in."

The same could be said of the Andalusians or Lusitanos fighting the bull.

These three examples show the importance of the process of "tipping under" of the "pelvic table" in establishing balance.

The example of the Quarterhorse, however, is a little more compelling, since the Quarterhorse is capable of displaying the "tucking in" not only when he decelerates, as with the European horses I have mentioned, but also when he accelerates, which gives him the edge over them. To the extent that perfecting a horse's balance is the

[4]

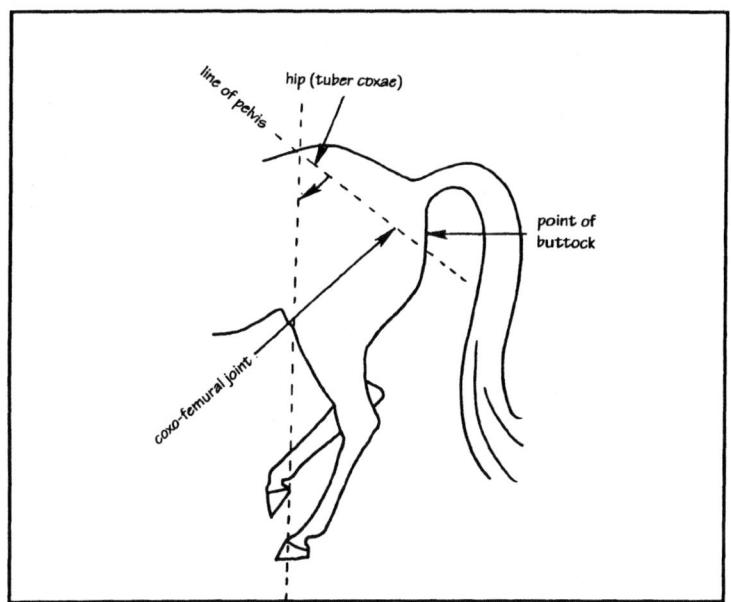

Fig. 1 - Slanting the pelvis..

purpose of dressage training, developing this ability of a horse to "tuck in" his haunches and keep them "tucked in" as he proceeds forward should be its primary goal (Fig. 1).

Lifting the withers

Thirty years ago, as I was looking out the window at this one horse that was standing in the yard, I was struck by the impression that he was taller than I thought. I checked immediately and found out that he had grown one inch and a half in one year.

Now that growth was very difficult to explain, since it was about a six-year-old "trotter" (French equivalent for "standard bred"); these horses are fed in a very efficient manner, they race at an early age, and for both reasons have terminated their growth around the age of five, if not before. In addition to that, I knew that he had been castrated late, one more reason for his having reached his definitive size at an earlier age.

That horse was a very good jumper, but obviously some retraining on the flat had been necessary to make a jumper out of a horse who had been trained only to trot, i.e., for which canter was a sin. This retraining, of course, had aimed at giving him more "collection."

I concluded that more than likely, this increase in size could not be explained physiologically by a growth of the spinous processes of the vertebrae of the withers, but by a strengthening of the muscles which carry the rib cage between the shoulder blades, resulting in a permanent lifting of this very rib cage.

This did not come as a surprise to me, since I knew that a horse has no clavicle, making this lifting of the rib cage more plausible. I had become aware of that anatomic particularity by reading Chapter V of General Decarpentry's **Academic Equitation**, devoted to the "lifting of the head." In this chapter, General Decarpentry contends that, because a horse has no clavicle, lifting his head will result in the sinking of the withers between the shoulder blades, for, he says, the cervical vertebrae push onto one another, from the first, the "atlas," down to the seventh, next to the rib cage.

I was beholden to General Decarpentry for giving me this piece of information about the missing clavicle, but I was shocked about his using it to dismiss the utility of the elevation of the neck, and this for two reasons:

First, I knew that General Decarpentry had been a great admirer of Captain Etienne Beudant, the most brilliant of the Baucherists of the second "manner" (in private conversations, he had dubbed him "flabbergasting"). Now Beudant was a staunch proponent of the lifting of the neck. It seemed to me that Decarpentry's stance had more to do with "political correctness" than with genuineness.

Secondly, I thought, if due to the absence of bony attachment of the rib cage to the shoulder blades, the withers can sink, they certainly can also rise. Or was I the only rider whose horses would at times raise their withers in front of the saddle?

Then it dawned on me that because of the absence of rigidity in the connection between shoulder blades and rib cage, a horse's size would probably shrink as he was mounted. I took measurements and found out that the average loss of height, between a horse un-

Fig. 2 - Lifting the withers by lifting the head.

[7]

mounted and the same horse mounted under a weight of 150 pounds, equalled two thirds of an inch. This alone could explain why a horse, so graceful at liberty, would sometimes become so clumsy when mounted. So the task of training, if balance was our purpose, was to teach a horse how to lift his withers when mounted, in order to annul the noxious effects of his rider's weight. In this respect, collection, with its effect on lifting the front end of a horse, was no longer a constraint, but on the contrary a liberation.

I did another experiment. Setting my horses on a cement slab, to avoid any uncertainty in the measurements, I took their size as they were munching hay on the ground, then as they were holding their heads at a standard height, and then when their heads were lifted to a maximum, and I found three different measures, in a growing order (Fig. 2). This showed that General Decarpentry, at best, had been mistaken.

One cannot emphasize too much the importance of the elevation of the withers. It is a necessary complement to the flexion of the pelvis, as it is in part responsible for it being useful. By "tucking in" his pelvis, a horse uplifts his spinal column, hence his withers. If the withers cannot rise, this uplifting of the vertebral column is made impossible. Thus is the flexion of the pelvis made more difficult, and less profitable.

Therefore the elevation of the withers is a "sine qua non" condition for any good horsemanship.

[8]

The "ramener"

The "ramener," in the French riding terminology, is the classical head set; it is characterized by the verticality of the forehead, with the poll the highest point of the upper line (Fig. 3).

In 1954, I was assigned to a Regiment in Tunisia, then a French protectorate. For the first time, I was confronted with the second "manner" of Baucher, since Colonel de Champvalliers, commanding the Cavalry in Tunisia, was an ardent supporter of this school of thought. More or less of their free will, all his staff officers would work their horses along the same lines.

An important feature of the second "manner" is the lifting of the horse's head. I was not in the least impressed by this technique, until a horse I was riding, upon raising his head in an evasion, offered a "passage" I was not asking for (and that he had not been trained for).

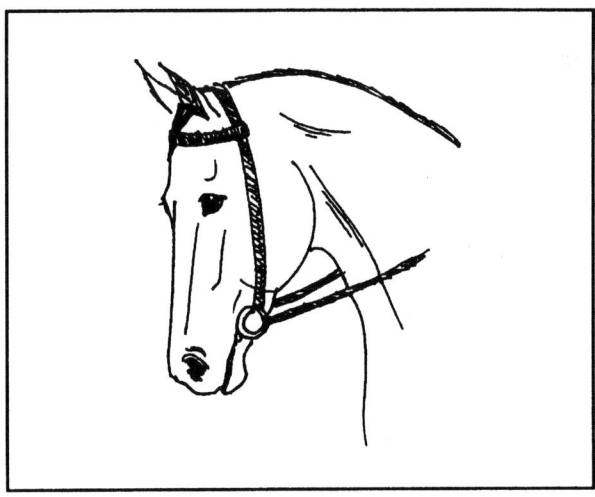

*Fig. 3 - The **ramener**.*

This showed me that balance as well as impulsion could proceed from the elevation of the neck. I have related the whole story in detail in my book **Racinet explains Baucher.**

I decided then that I would try to use this technique for the next horse I would have to train, which happened to be an Algerian "Barb," since I was subsequently assigned to a Regiment in Algeria. In no time, this horse was passaging, and I had got this result through elevating his neck.

Once, a photograph of me and my horse was taken, as we were passaging, and I was very surprised by the academic "ramener" of my horse, a result that I had not tried to achieve, and which looked to be a very unlikely consequence of the lifting of the neck. This confirmed me, at the time, in the idea that the "ramener" should happen as a consequence of collection, as with Baucher's "second manner", and not as its prerequisite, as with Baucher in his "first manner".

I have to mention that General Decarpentry, after having asserted that the lifting of the head sinks the withers between the shoulders, somewhat corrects this statement by adding that the "ramener" added to the lifting of the head takes care of this problem. Beudant thinks otherwise, since he wrote that "the 'ramener' is not necessary for balance." And, of course, there cannot be balance if the withers are sunken between the shoulders.

But one can perhaps conciliate these two opposing views by saying that if it cannot be proven that the "ramener" creates ipso facto the conditions for balance, that is, the elevation of the withers and the "tipping under" of the pelvis, it certainly confirms them, when they have been obtained through the elevation of the neck.

For this to happen, the ramener has to be afforded freely by the horse, so that the horse will put his muscles to work and not his rider's, which rules out any forced attitude which, however "pretty" to the onlooker, does not give one the assurance that the right muscles are going to work as they should.

Therefore ramener should always be coupled with lightness.

The flexion of the jaw

Back in Europe after seven years in Tunisia and Algeria, I tried to translate to our warmbloods the techniques which had worked so well in North Africa with the "Barbs," but they happened to be much less convincing, and I looked for "something else." I found it in the "flexion of the jaw." I used it first with prudence, then with hope, then with enthusiasm, and have never been let down by it. Using the technique of the "impulsive flexion," which I have described in many articles and books (see **Another Horsemanship** and **Racinet Explains Baucher**), I taught twenty-five horses or thereabout the passage, and to a lesser number the piaffe and passage.

Masterpiece of Baucherism, the flexion of the jaw amounts to a relaxation of the temporo-mandibular joint. If the lower jaw yields in a mellow way at the rider's request, we are assured that there does not remain any tension in the TMJ area. This in turn, as has been shown time and again, is a token for balance.

At the beginning of his equestrian quest, Baucher believed that the "ramener," simply defined as the verticality of the head, was the "sine qua non" condition for balance. This "ramener" was the result of the "direct" (that is, fore and aft) flexion of the neck. It was prepared by diverse lateral flexions. Each flexion would be considered as done when, upon being properly bent in his neck, the horse would "chew his bit." This was also the rule for the direct flexion; it would not be done without a "chewing of the bit" (more in Appendix 1).

Then Baucher focused more and more on this "chewing," giving it a more and more sophisticated definition: jaw flexion, mobility of the jaw, yielding of the jaw...In his "second manner", the jaw flexion would not end and validate the direct flexion; it was called for independently and should not entail any movement of the head. The "ramener," or direct flexion, would then be the result of the horse being worked in the forward movement after he had yielded in his jaw (more in Appendix 2).

What was interesting for me in the flexion of the jaw was its character of absolute necessity. Each time I tried to do without it, I was obliged to come back to it, irrespective of the lowness of the result I would have drawn from it. We all want one hundred percent success in our training. Supposing that I got only twenty percent using the flexion of the jaw; I would have got only ten percent doing without it.

The posture

From a rider's point of view, two distinct muscular functions preside over the equestrian performance. The first function assures locomotion. It is acted out through an alternation of extensions and contractions.

The second function must establish favorable articular angles and provide a fulcrum to the action of the muscles in charge of the first function. It upholds the structure. In one word, it assures the "posture." This second function works through a steady muscular tension.

It is obvious that the muscles affected by the first function, which requires an intermittent tension, cannot in the meantime fulfill the second function, which requires a steady tension. Therefore the two

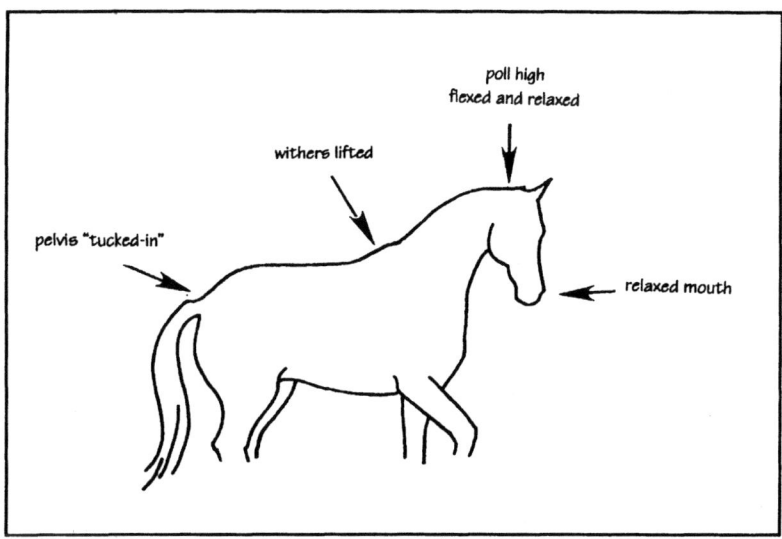

*Fig. 4 - The **posture**.*

muscle sets affected by either function are, at any given time, totally distinct. Their definition is, however, blurred, since in plain, day-to-day riding, at a walk or at a gallop or over the jumps, the posture constantly changes.

At a trot, however, the posture is steady; the head position as well as the angle of the pelvis is pretty constant. At a trot, even at a racing trot, the horse's body is, so to say, "gelled"; its form does not change.

This characteristic is also present with the other gaits in superior, collected horsemanship. Therefore in this equitation the muscular system in charge of assuring posture is perfectly defined and distinct from the system affording locomotion "per se."

From all that has been stated so far, we can deduce that the posture which will create the total balance will combine the "tipping under" of the haunches with the lifting of the withers (by the elevation of the neck) and the flexion of the poll (ramener), the flexion of the jaw being the cornerstone of the edifice (Fig. 4). This posture is called "collection" (more in Appendix 3).

Two different horsemanships

In dressage, or more broadly superior, academic horsemanship, the development of the muscular system in charge of locomotion for the sheer sake of itself, as with racing or endurance riding horses, is not of the essence. On the contrary, the goal of dressage work is essentially to perfect the efficacy of the other system, that which affords the posture, inasmuch as, in this type of horsemanship, this system is well defined. In other words, the purpose of dressage training is to muscle up the horse so that he will easily assume the right "posture," that is, by and large, that which allows a balance "on the haunches."

Starting from this observation, there exist two roads to attain the said goal. The first one consists of targeting system #1 (posture) by setting to work system #2 (locomotion). In other words, with this method, balance is sought through movement. The more the movement becomes difficult, the more the horse will have to perfect his balance, hence strengthen and "educate" the first system of muscles. Balance is the end goal, not the prerequisite. Movement is the prerequisite.

The posture being, so to say, "evolvable," "modular," this philosophy will impart to every level of movement no more than its required part of "posture." The fully trained horse, when performing a movement of a lower level, will be required to revert to the degree of posture he could only afford when he was being trained at that level. In plain English, full collection will be required from the horse only for some rare and slow movements, total balance not being looked for in any other circumstance.

The notions of transitions, contact, and half-halts are central to this method. Transitions teach a horse to evolve along the gamut of the different postures leading to the supreme one, when the horse is fully collected. Contact is necessary to apply half-halts without jolts. Half-halts reset a horse on the haunches.

In this equitation, the horses should be constantly collectable. Its motto is: "permeability."

In many respects this conception is that of the "classical," baroque era, and is still enforced by the FEI nowadays.

The second road consists of targeting muscular system #1 (posture) directly, by establishing balance first, and introducing movement little by little, and only to the extent that this does not alter the balance. Balance is the prerequisite, movement is not. With this method, of course, there is only one balance throughout the progression, hence, one posture; the horse is set on the haunches not only to perform a piaffe but an extended trot as well. Transitions are no longer an issue; they are mere result, since they are made easy by the fact that balance remains unaltered. With the fully trained horse, there is no more need for half-halts. Lightness of the jaw is the guarantee that balance will not be lost, whichever the speed or extension of the gait.

In this equitation, the horse is constantly collected. Its motto is: "lightness."

This conception is "Baucherist."

Critique of the FEI conception

It is obvious that if one asks a young horse with three weeks under the saddle to perform tempi flying changes, he will not do it. A progression is therefore necessary to school a horse, that is, to instruct him, to speak to his intellect.

But can the same horse, ideally, physically perform these tempi flying changes? Certainly : watch him play in a pasture. Watch children as they play: do they need athletic training to be able to "skip"?

So, has the dressage progression much meaning as concerns the physical ability of the horse to perform increasingly more difficult movements? I don't think so.

Try this simple experiment: as you are walking a free walk down the centerline, position your weight to the right and stick your right leg, near the girth, against the horse's side. Nothing will happen. Then, keeping your weight to the right and your right leg against the horse, progressively slow the pace; all of a sudden, the horse will proceed sideways to the left.

What made the difference is that, by slowing down, you have set the horse in a balance allowing him to move sideways, which he couldn't do at a free walk.

This shows that it is the rider who has to establish the balance necessary for a given movement; the horse will certainly not do it of his own initiative. Yet that is what the FEI conception postulates when it expects to perfect balance through movement.

How come a few horses end up performing at Grand Prix level? It is because they had, at the onset of their training, the required balance to become Grand Prix horses; they have not acquired it. What they have acquired is the intellectual knowledge of what they are required to do, and of course some physical habits as well.

So the system of horsemanship which makes movement a prerequisite and balance a consequence is only a system of progressive selection of good horses.

This system was certainly justified in baroque times, because it was the nobility that was riding, and it needed a horse for war, and war is very taxing on horses. So the physical aspect of training, movement for its own sake, was to be stressed. On the other hand, the problem of balance was more than half solved in advance by the choice of the horses, who were all from Iberian, Barb, or the like stock. Those horses have a naturally good balance. Moreover, the aristocratic conception that prevailed for the humans was projected to the horses as well: only the "noble" horses were worked, the others being left, in La Guérinière's words, "to the whims of their nature and the routine of the teamsters."

It has been often said that the introduction of the Thoroughbred on the European market after the fall of Napoleon explains the "Baucher phenomenon." Built for speed, the Thoroughbred would not lend itself easily to the old methods of training. But there is probably another reason, more compelling, that lies in the paucity of good saddle horses at that time in France. So the matter was not to take advantage of the balance of the horses present on the market; it was to give them some if possible.

Baucherism: means and philosophy

Throughout his life, Baucher varied widely as concerns the means he would use. He started with the "effet d'ensemble," a plain opposition of hand and legs, and ended up preaching "hand without legs, legs without hand." He started depressing his horse's neck and ended up lifting it. He started using "diagonal aids" (hand and leg diagonally opposed) and ended up using lateral aids, condemning the former. He started using outright lateral flexions of the neck and ended up practicing only semi-lateral flexions. Etc...

But he never wavered in his philosophy.

This philosophy can be summed up in this way:

1) Balance comes prior to movement.
2) Balance is established at a halt, or at slow gaits, and then tested in movement.
3) In motion, the yielding of the jaw acknowledges and maintains balance.

While the central notion, as far as the training philosophy is concerned, lies in the primacy of balance, the central tool for getting this balance remains the yielding of the jaw. This is probably why, on his deathbed, Baucher said to his friend the future General L'Hotte: "Remember well, L'Hotte: always this [and he pressed L'Hotte's hand in his]; never that [and he pulled L'Hotte's hand toward his chest]." This, which sums up the principle of "the fixed hand," is, as it happens, the way to obtain flexions of the jaw from a horse.

In Baucher's first "manner," the flexion of the jaw sanctions the flexion of the neck; it is the icing on the cake. Progressively, though,

Baucher focussed more and more on this jaw flexion, up to making it the prerequisite to any neck flexion in his second "manner."

This applied to the lateral flexions of neck, but as much if not more to the "direct flexion," that is, a fore and aft flexion of the neck. In the first "manner," the "ramener," or direct flexion, was more or less obtained through force, and then (but only then) the mouth would be invited to yield. In the second "manner," on the contrary, the yielding of the jaw is asked for irrespective of the position of the head, which it should not alter. If this yielding of the jaw is obtained after the horse's head has been lifted, then the head will, of its own movement, and upon the rider's giving with the hand, "fall" in a vertical or thereabout direction.

This process is called "mise en main" ("bringing in hand"). It is a combination of "ramener" and "yielding of the jaw," a "ramener" obtained through (and not prior to) the flexion of the jaw (Fig. 5).

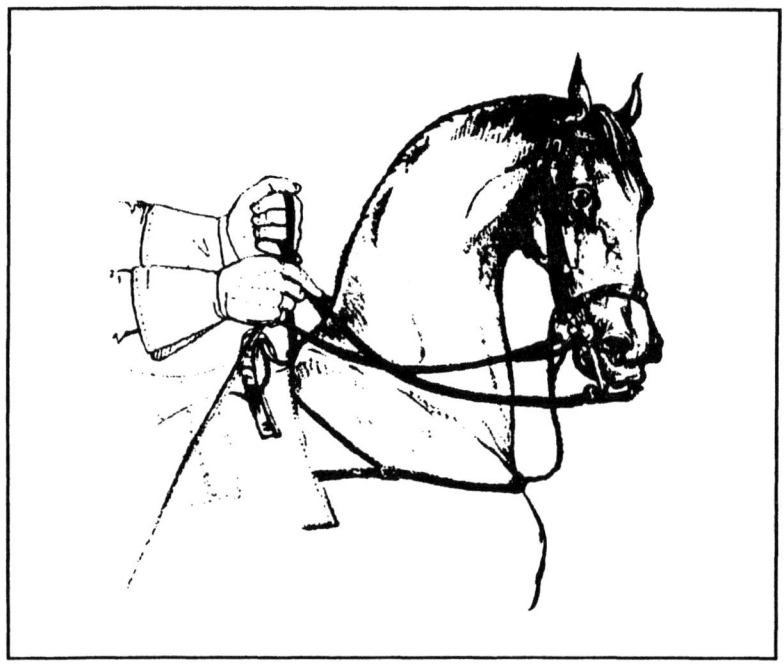

*Fig. 5 - The **mise en main**.*

And here comes the central part of Baucherism's "second man-
ner" and of this book as well: with a sound horse, that is, a horse
devoid of any major vertebral blocking (an aspect which will be
amply developed in the following chapters), **the "mise en main"**
("bringing in hand") **is the necessary and sufficient condition for**
total collection, that is, for establishing the one and only bal-
ance *(which Baucher called of the "first genre")* **which will preside**
over all the evolutions of the horse. *(The rider's legs are not*
involved; they only give the "go".)

When the poll is high (the highest point), flexed and relaxed
(through the jaw flexion), the two other components of collection,
which are the lifting of the withers and the flexion of the haunches,
are ipso-facto realized.

Obstacles to the "mise en main"

A few horses will give the jaw flexion willingly and easily without preparation, but most won't. This most often, results from incomprehension or stiffness or both. That's why the jaw flexion has to be taught to a horse.

But it may happen that, in spite of all the efforts of the trainer, the result remains incomplete. The horse certainly flexes his jaw, but does not relax his TMJ very much, which is the goal of this technique.

Until the recent past, this was an impossible problem to solve; it could only be skirted around. Remaining imperfect, the flexion of jaw would yield imperfect results. So either the horse would gape in his jaw, or he would be a little too "talkative," or noisy (which was a mark of irritation more than a mark of contentment), or he would not raise his withers as much as he should have, and the hind legs had to be brought under artificially, by using a whip in the work in hand. But while this would shrink the base of support and bring some relief to the weight carried by the front legs, this would not produce a flexion of the sacro-lumbar joint; the flexion would be staged only at the level of the "coxo-femural" joint, the joint between femur and pelvis.

This, of course, brought many critics upon Baucher's theories, but the fact remains that any other method would not have worked better in establishing balance with such a horse, since the snag was out of reach of any known method. In fact, they would have worked even less well, which is what I explained as I spoke of the character of "absolute necessity" of the jaw flexion, a jaw flexion that would not always deliver all we were expecting from it, but still more than would have been obtained in its absence.

So where was the snag lying?

I have found out, without a shadow of a doubt, that the snag lies in vertebral blockings, which may happen with the cervical vertebrae, and the thoracic vertebrae as well, more so in the front part of the thoracic segment of the vertebral column.

I have also found out that the lateral flexions of jaw (flexions of neck coupled with a jaw yielding) may release vertebral blockings in the front part of the horse, from C1 ("atlas," "C" stands for "cervical") to as far as T3, the third thoracic vertebra. And this is a blatant vindication of Baucher's inspired intuition.

Vertebral blockings situated further back, anywhere from T4 to L6, the sixth lumbar vertebra, may also prevent a horse from lifting his withers correctly, if at all; flexing the jaw will then be of little avail, which is a reason why this technique has not received the recognition it deserves.

This leads me to broaden the scope of this exposé.

PART TWO

THE ANTITHESIS

Introducing Dr. Giniaux

The French veterinarian Dominique Giniaux, D.V.M., studied human osteopathy with Dr. Jean Josse, a certified osteopath in human medicine, and he translated this knowledge from the humans to horses, dogs, and cats. He was the first to establish the chart defining the pathology linked to the diverse vertebral lesions in the equine. In 1987, he published a book, **Les Chevaux m'ont dit**, whose English translation was published in 1996, under the title of **What the Horses Have Told Me** by Xenophon Press.

Osteopathy was founded in 1874 by Andrew Taylor Still. This new, holistic science postulated that if all the joints of an organism, not only bony joints but fascias as well (fascias are those pearly envelopes which wrap up every muscle), are enjoying their normal range of motion, the individual will be in good health, the "energy" (nervous energy and blood flow) will circulate normally.

There are two types of osteopaths.

"Structural" osteopaths, like Dr. Giniaux, focus on vertebral problems, although not exclusively. Their manipulations present a "mechanical" aspect. "Fluidic" osteopaths work on the premises established by W.G. Sutherland who, in 1937, discovered the "primordial respiration," i.e., the fact that the cerebro-spinal liquid is animated by a pulse, which translates into a rhythmic deformation of the skull, whose bones are no longer considered inanimate. Their main technique is called "sacro-cranial" therapy, since it compares the pulse of the cerebro-spinal fluid at the levels of the sacrum and skull. Sacro-cranial manipulations are rendered very difficult with the horse because of its size.

American riders are more aware of the existence of chiropractors than of structural osteopaths. Both target the vertebral lesions, but they tend to diverge on the nature of the lesion, and on its manipulation. "Subluxation" is the name given to the lesion by chiropractors. They believe that it is about a subliminal dislocation, mechanically induced, which will be taken care of by directly realigning the concerned vertebrae. The osteopaths prefer to speak of "vertebral blocking." They stress the loss of mobility of the vertebrae. They believe that this loss of mobility is induced by a nervous spasm at the level of the intervertebral muscles surrounding the vertebrae, as a reaction to some situation of crisis: the brain "at large," that is, the intelligence which presides over the functioning of the nervous system, reacts by immobilizing, "blocking," the segment of the vertebral column threatened by the trauma.

This protective reaction, meant to prevent further damage, then becomes the main pathological agent, since Nature doesn't seem to know how to lower its guard and never sends any message of "end of alarm."

The osteopathic manipulations are indirect: they aim at releasing the muscular spasm, through adequate flexions, and then if the vertebra comes back to "alignment," it is of its own movement.

Whether one chooses to call them subluxations or blockings, the vertebral lesions can no longer be ignored by the riders, since they are the "missing link" which explains the poor results obtained on some horses by the best riding methods. They will allow us to eliminate all the uncertainties which still remain in the riding theories.

Although their incidence on the pathology of the organs belongs entirely to veterinary art and responsibility, their noxious influence in the field of posture and locomotion can be considered an aspect of horsemanship broadly understood - hence the title of this book.

It is situated at the border between veterinary art and equitation, which will certainly create conflicts of attribution, but it certainly concerns the art of riding and dressage training in its daily application. For instance, nobody would think of calling the veterinarian because they cannot correctly perform a half pass to the right. Now it so happens that in most cases, such a difficulty finds its origin in a blocked vertebra (in this case most likely T1). And there are cases of lameness that sometimes cannot be dealt with properly by the veterinarians (in the actual state of their training) and might be solved by a simple manipulation which, being a flexion, belongs entirely in the domain of equitation.

Besides, as I shall demonstrate further on, Baucher himself was an unwitting structural osteopath.

Manipulations: Three laws, plus one

Vertebral displacements, as such, are extremely rare. Those are displacements that exceed the normal range of motion of the vertebra. But within this range of motion, a vertebra can occupy several positions: it can rotate slightly around an imaginary horizontal axis placed at the center of the medullary canal (where the spinal cord rests), it can go slightly up and down, perhaps one millimeter, perhaps less. When a vertebra is blocked, it is "locked" in one of those positions (hence the word "subluxation"). The purpose of the manipulations is to unlock the vertebra and allow it to retrieve its mobility within its natural range of motion.

The principle of the osteopathic manipulations as described by Dr. Giniaux is reminiscent of homeopathy, whereby "like treats like." Instead of pushing the vertebra back toward its position of balance (chiropractic manipulations), which amounts to "fighting" the spasm, it aims at moving the vertebra in the other direction, away from its position of balance. Going "with" and not against the spasm deceives and releases it.

Law #1: Law of the handbrake

This can be summed up under the heading of "law of the handbrake," since it is exactly what happens when we have to unlock a handbrake in a truck or a car. We do not push it immediately toward the direction of release, but on the contrary, we "pull" as if we wanted to tighten the brake still more; only this allows us to release the "ratchet" mechanism which was blocking the handbrake.

This movement of the vertebra away from its position of balance is created by the ad hoc flexion of the horse's body or neck.

The direction of this flexion is given by a law which I call the "tridimensional law":

Experience shows that if one tries to laterally bend a horse's body (thoraco-lumbar segment), the possibilities of bending are rapidly saturated. But if one manages to provoke a "rotation" of the vertebral column around its horizontal axis, the possibilities of lateral flexion increase noticeably. And here comes the law:

Law #2: "Tridimensional" law

• If the rotation goes outwardly with respect to the lateral flexion, the vertebral column will tend to display a convex profile (will "round" itself);

• If the rotation goes inwardly, the vertebral column will tend to display a concave profile (will "hollow" itself).

Thus there are two very important "triads," which should be constantly borne in mind when one wants to manipulate:

"outward rotation, inward bending, convexity"

and

"inward rotation, inward bending, concatvity"

(see Fig. 6).

With each triad, establishing two elements will entail the coming up of the third. For instance, if we create outward rotation and inward bending, convexity will ensue. If we create outward rotation and convexity, inward bending will ensue. And if we create inward bending and convexity, outward rotation will ensue.

The same for the other "triad."

I could not insist too much on the necessity of understanding clearly this phenomenon, and on keeping a vivid image of it in one's mind. Otherwise, dangerous errors can happen: dangerous for the

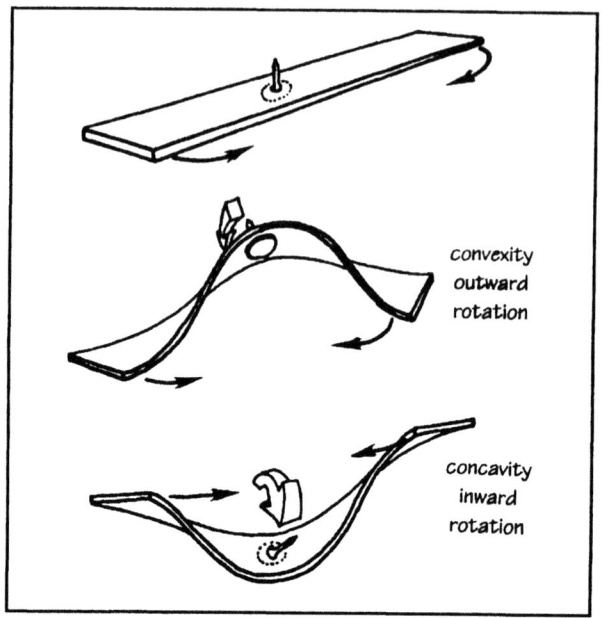

*Fig. 6 - The **tridimentional law.***
(Diagram reproduced from Dr. Giniaux's Whate the
Horses Have Told Me, with the author's permission.)

horse because fighting the spasm, instead of deceiving it, may hurt; dangerous as well for the rider, by reasons of the inconsiderate and violent reactions a horse can display when it hurts.

Law #3: "The horse is always right"

Then a third law comes into play: it states that "the horse is always right." In other words, one should carefully examine the horse's reactions, its "body language." Nothing is to be overlooked. For instance, it sometimes happens that when one comes closer to a horse on one side, the side where we intend to manipulate, the horse moves away from us. It would be an error to ask somebody to stand on the other side in order to force him to stay put. The horse was sending us a message that we have to take into consideration. Horses have a body awareness that we humans have lost long ago.

Observation should be very careful, of the way the horse engages or disengages one hind leg or both, of the way he places the track of his hind legs behind the track of his front legs, the way his withers rise or don't by each step of walk forward, the depth of the backing up gesture of his front legs as he reins back, etc...

I shall give hereunder an example of the way those laws can combine.

If a lumbar vertebra seems offset to the right, for instance, the first law, that of the "handbrake", will dictate that we try to make it move more to the right.

To make this happen, the tridimensional law will tell us to bend the horse to the left and to increase the already convex curvature of the lumbar segment.

But if this bending to the left and this increase of the convexity seem impossible to obtain, the body resisting the manipulation, then you know that you are wrong. Don't fight nature; that's always an error. The horse's body is sending you a message. Try to understand, palpate again in order to find the explanation of this behavior, etc...

This is exactly what happened to me with my horse "Flambard." He was afflicted with a strong blocking of his first lumbar vertebra to the right. But as he was walking, he was bringing his croup quite markedly to the right (whereas one could have expected the croup to be offset to the left, since the lumbar segment is naturally convex). In the meantime, he was not engaging his rear end, an indication that the spasm was hollowing his back. So I manipulated by bending the horse to the right, whilst I hollowed his back by lifting the tail. This took care of the problem, but also allowed me to come up with a fourth law:

Law #4: "The logic of the spasm overcomes the logic of the segment"

There may be spasms whose nature are "concave," like the one I mentioned, although they are situated on a convex segment. It means that they withhold the vertebra sideways and downwards at the same time. To "deceive" them, one has to go in the direction of their traction, i.e., downwards and sideways. But if we had followed the logic of the segment, we would have bent in the other direction and increased the already convex curvature of the segment. That would have been an error; that would have meant fighting the spasm by pulling against it, instead of deceiving it by moving the vertebra in its direction.

All that has been said in the lines above is most important. If you don't get it clearly, read it again, and reread it until you fully understand, because it would be of little avail to skip it and try to handle the question after a fashion, with no deep understanding of what you are doing.

Palpation

In his book, Dr. Giniaux advises riders to form the habit of "palpating" the horses' backs, all the horses that we can set a hand on, so as to "hone" our feel. He urges us to acquire the "sensitivity of a blind person," telling us that blind persons can read a text in Braille at the same speed as we read with our eyes. Now if we would pass our uneducated fingers along a text in Braille, we would hardly feel the "grain" it is made of.

But in the meantime, Dr. Giniaux does not describe any of his manipulations, lest he see people misusing them. There is, of course, a contradiction inherent in this view, for what avail can there be in "honing" one's perception for the sheer sake of it?

Yet Dr. Giniaux's apprehension underlines the importance palpation takes on.

The first thing to do is to look up in an equine anatomy book and get a clear picture of the organization of a horse's skeleton (Fig. 7). Note that the cervical vertebrae do not follow the crest of the horse's neck but are by and large nearer the throat.

Feeling the cervical vertebrae is easy, with the exception of the second cervical. The second cervical lies between the first and the third, which are both easy to locate. The first is right behind the horse's head, and its shape is unmistakable. The third lies in the alignment of the base of the horse's lower jaw, where this line crosses the neck.

What one feels, which so many riders mistake for a muscle (they even sometimes give shots in this area) are the lateral processes of the cervical vertebrae. They end up very close to the skin, and they build up those strong "knots" that people sometimes mistake for an

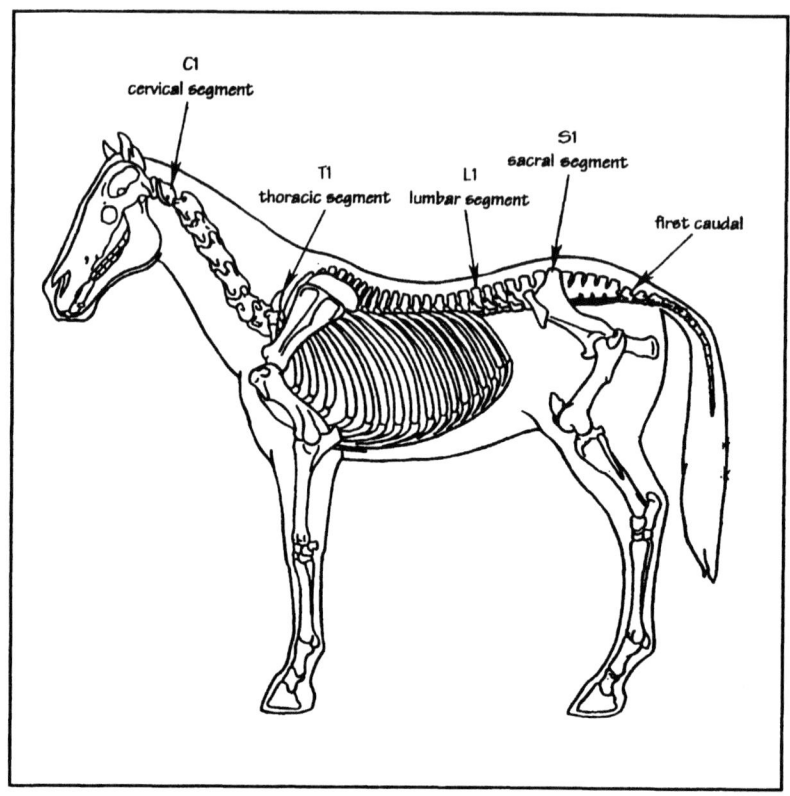

Fig. 7 - The horse's skeleton.
Cervical segment - 7 vertebrae; Thoracic degment - 18 vertebrae;
Lumbar segment - 6 vertebrae (5 with Arabians and Barbs);
Sacral segment - 5 fused vertebrae plus a triangular bone.

abnormal swelling. You should not hesitate to push rather strongly, more so at the level of the vertebral joints near the chest, to evaluate their "pliability." If you have a clear picture in mind of what you are looking for, you will find the right gesture.

We therefore can feel the cervical vertebrae down to the seventh, and its junction with the first thoracic. This latter cannot really be felt. The three first thoracic vertebrae are situated between the shoulder blades and cannot be felt, although practice will allow you in time to feel the tip top of the spinous process of the third vertebra, right under the cord of the nuchal ligament and in front of the withers.

The first vertebra to be felt in the withers' area is the fourth thoracic. Usually, the fifth thoracic marks the highest point of the withers. From the fifth to the tenth thoracic, there is no difficulty in feeling the spinous processes. The tenth (very often blocked, perhaps due to its proximity to the saddle) has often a sharp contour which helps to recognize it.

Further down the road, palpation becomes more difficult, because of the presence of the muscles on both sides of the vertebral column, all the more when it comes to palpating a dressage horse whose back has been muscled up through strong work. But then you will have an idea of the general position of a given vertebra through the relief of the said muscles at this level (Webster's: relief: the elevations or inequalities of a land surface"). You may feel the slightest deviation to the right or the left. The side of the deviation should appear slightly lower than the other side, because of the rotation of the vertebral body. If the side of the deviation is higher than the other, then it means that there is probably both a rotation *in the other direction* and a slight displacement opposite to the direction of rotation. These cases happen sometimes at the level of the vertebrae under the saddle, or at the level of the lumbar. I have seen a horse display this particularity in his withers; needless to say, he was particularly stiff and sore.

In both cases, treat only the "rotation" problem.

The lumbar vertebrae are easy to feel, with the exception, sometimes, of the last one, the sixth. Their spinous processes are narrower and longer than those of the last thoracic vertebrae. Feeling the pelvis is utterly simple. You can assess its liberty by pushing softly on the hip; you should not get the impression of a "rock." Any blocking of the sacrum will translate into the same difficulty of the hips to yield to hand pressure.

A blocking of the sacrum, that is to say of the sacro-lumbar joint, will be evident by a neat rotation of the first sacral vertebra, which can be seen from the rear, added to a lack of tension in the muscles on the lower side, creating a kind of "dent" next to the "hunter bump" and some sensitivity in this area. However, not all the cases in which a horse displays some unevenness in his behind are amenable to a pelvis problem. A horse is a whole, and I have seen more than once blockings as far as the first thoracic entail a rotation of the pelvis.

Generally, the blocking of a vertebra from C1 to L6 is relatively simple to spot. You have to push laterally onto the lateral process (for a cervical vertebra) or the spinous process (for all the other vertebrae) and feel whether they "give." That "give" should be little but very neat. Vertebrae should "give" in both directions. Usually (sometimes with the exception of the cervical vertebrae, which may appear to be blocked bilaterally), a vertebra which does not "give" on one side will "give" on the other side, and you then get a first idea of the nature of the spasm.

A blocking of C1 (atlas) is felt in this way: if you are on the left side of the horse, set your right hand on the lateral process of this vertebra (it takes on the shape of a "wing"; besides, it is called the wing of the atlas), without pushing, only resisting, and pull the horse's head laterally, using the inside rein. There should be a "give" at the level of the (apparent) junction of the jowl with the wing of the atlas, allowing the head to "rotate" as if the matter was to "unscrew" it from the neck. If there is no give, and/or if there is a fight, no doubt there is a blocking at this level. This palpation is bilateral.

Many horses have their "atlanto-occipital" joint blocked. It is to be observed that, upon being manipulated, if those horses are worked according to the principles of lightness, that is, through jaw flexions, this blocking never comes back.

Strong blockings of the atlas sometimes entail a rotation of this vertebra, which can be assessed by measuring on both sides the width of the "groove" between the jowl and the wing of the atlas. Minor blockings of the atlas are sometimes linked to a blocking of the haunch on the same side.

Severe blockings of the atlas are almost always linked (and due to) a blocking of the sixth or fifth lumbar vertebra. They create troubles of the vision, fear, and anxiety, and a propensity to "spook" and rear.

Note that a blocking of the sixth, and to a lesser extent of the fifth, lumbar vertebra is likely to entail trouble with urination (cf. Dr. Giniaux, op. cit.).

A blocking of the second thoracic vertebra cannot be felt, but it always entails a tension and sometimes some bulging in the area of the splenius or the serratus ventralis cervicis next to the shoulder. You will note that this tension disappears completely after manipulation.

A blocking of the third thoracic vertebra can be felt by a lateral tension in the area of the cord of the nuchal ligament, next to the withers. The tip of the spinous process of the third vertebra can be felt, laterally, and its mobility assessed. This requires some practice.

When the track of the horse's front legs is too narrow, giving the impression that the horse crosses over slightly when he walks, one can be assured that the third thoracic vertebra is blocked. Releasing this spasm takes care of this problem, and the track of the front legs comes back to normalcy.

Often, when the third thoracic vertebra is blocked, the horse keeps his head high; he does not correctly engage his hind legs and seems to more or less "hop" with the hindquarters as he canters. Under the saddle, such a blocking may be very painful and trigger off dangerous reactions (see further on "the Géricault case").

Local heat can be an indication, as can an unexpected sensitivity; a horse should not arch his back too briskly as we run our fingers on the top of his spinal column (watch out for your nails!).

To evaluate the nature of a spasm ("convex" or "concave"), attentively watch the line of the spinal column: although it may look convex, and even more so if you push the back up by pressing your fingers or a hoof pick under the belly, you may possibly spot a little "dent" at the level of the blocking, telling you that there is a "concave" spasm.

As a matter of fact, with our horses (dressage, jumping, or trail horses), the vast majority of the spasms are of a "concave" nature, probably because we pound on their poor backs. With racehorses, whose backs' sagittal suppleness is surprising (they can round their backs like greyhounds), one will more often acknowledge "convex" blockings. Read what Dr. Giniaux says of the racehorses, who have a great propensity to blocking their second lumbar vertebra (op. cit.). (Besides, you should not read this book without reading Dr. Giniaux's as well).

Probable causes for vertebral blockings

In the light of what we know now, and since the vertebral blockings interfere so much with equestrian performance, one wonders how in the world the basic principles of equitation can ever have been established. Now, they were. Does that mean that those vertebral problems do not fundamentally affect the equestrian reality, that they are only a minor hindrance? Not in the least. It just means that riding theories were established on good horses. In the baroque era, almost all the riding authors belonged to the nobility, and the nobility would not remount itself with bad horses. In the following centuries, almost all the riding authors, with the noticeable exception of Baucher, were coming from the military, and the officers would always remount themselves with the best. When a horse was easy, noble, athletic, and elegant, he would be called an "officer's horse."

That's why all the riding theories always work for the mounts of Olympic champions but won't work for your gangly Thoroughbred, your jigging Morgan, your stargazing Arabian, your gaited American Saddlebred, your calm (how calm, indeed) Quarterhorse, your stubborn Appaloosa (but isn't it redundant to speak of a "stubborn Appaloosa"?), etc.

So what is a good horse? A good horse is a horse who, out of sheer luck, has avoided major vertebral problems and who, out of athletic ability, can work around the minor ones he has. This is why good horses are randomly found in all the breeds.

As I was giving a clinic in Oregon, I came across this Andalusian mare that was so crooked in her back that she would back up with a circular movement; her owner could not make her back up straight, and as for myself, I was obliged to carry both hands far to the right in order to get the desired result.

Now, the lady would not let me practice my "flexion-relaxations" on the mare. Yet it so happened that by the end of this three day clinic, she (the mare, not the lady) would back up straight, not only with me, but with her usual rider as well. Her body had adapted, probably at the cost of a few more vertebral compensations, but the fact remains that she was no longer crooked. There is a good horse, a horse riding theories have been made for (and from).

All horses display vertebral blockings. A wound received at an early age may have produced scar tissue, which may result in a limitation of the muscular suppleness on one side of the horse. Although Nature has a great power of adaptation, the horse will be more or less crooked on one side. Since the longissimi dorsi are hooked on the four last cervical vertebrae, C4, C5, C6, and C7, there will be, at the level of these vertebrae, a constant traction, which, in case of a "stress," may translate into vertebral blockings.

There are a host of other reasons.

A horse cast in his stall will have vertebral blockings. The exuberant horse who, as you turn him out in a pasture, darts all at once and slips in the mud will have vertebral blockings. A broodmare who just foaled will have vertebral problems. A gelding with scar tissue around his castration incision will have vertebral problems. A mare with difficult heats will have vertebral problems. A highly emotional horse will have vertebral problems. A worrier will have vertebral problems. A horse who has caught his hip in the door post of the stall will have vertebral problems. A horse who has panicked in the cross ties and pulled onto his halter, whether he broke it or not, will have vertebral problems. A horse who has been taught how to "bow" may have vertebral problems. A horse whose saddle does not fit will have vertebral problems. A horse trained with side reins, draw reins, and the like will have vertebral problems. A horse pushed onto his bit so that he will lower his head and take a strong contact will have vertebral problems. A horse who has been forced in a half pass or a counter-canter will have vertebral problems.

Shoeing can be another source of such troubles, but I don't want to add the farriers to the already too long list of my enemies. Shoeing is physically taxing and dangerous. Farriers are highly skilled specialists; we could not do without them. Yet they carry a heavy responsibility, because a traction on one leg in the wrong direction, more so if the horse gets panicky, may do the harm. It is why the good farrier will choose, most often, not to fight.

Let me develop some of these points.

• Two factors concur in creating vertebral blockings: a torsion or flexion of some sort coupled to a stress. Those two ingredients are present in the case of a horse cast in his stall. Soon after the incident, perhaps only one vertebra will have been blocked, but a whole chain of compensations will rapidly settle in. The consequences may be varied, depending on the setting of the lesions. If the 15th thoracic vertebra was blocked, the horse will lose his forward movement, and he will sweat abnormally as you work him (cf. Dr. Giniaux, op. cit.). If the first thoracic vertebra was involved, the horse will suddenly be reluctant to canter on a given lead. If the 12th thoracic was hit, then the horse will yawn constantly and either lose his appetite or on the contrary eat like an ogre, and perhaps some day he will become a "wind sucker" (the 12th thoracic is linked to stomach troubles; cf. Dr. Giniaux's book).

Very often, there will be some time between the incident and the emerging of the consequences, so that no obvious link can be established between the two; who would think, when their horse starts cribbing, that this may be due to his having been cast in his stall a few months ago? So we will think that the horse got "bored" of living in a stall; but why didn't he seem to be bored before?

• Broodmares, now. Mating is already a violent operation with the equine; gestation may be hard on the mare's back, but giving birth will be the icing on the cake. Most likely, being strained, the pelvis will be more or less displaced.

[43]

• Let's now mention castration problems. We are all aware of geldings who remain somewhat "studish." A possible explanation of the phenomenon is that scar tissues provoked by the incision of castration act like a gland and secrete some testosterone (explanation given to me by Dr. Giniaux).

Some geldings, as we palpate them, will erect suddenly. I have found out that five levels, at least, are involved in this process:

a) The sixth lumbar, because of its connection to the bladder. When it is blocked, the spasm propagates to the neck of the bladder, urination becomes difficult, and the horse retains his urine (cf. Dr. Giniaux, op. cit.). Now, a full bladder may foster erection.

b) The first lumbar, because it is linked to the sexual organs, ovaries with the mares and testicles with the stallions.

c) The first thoracic, quite much, because of its proximity to the "stellate ganglion," left of the first rib, a ganglion which is pretty much involved in all the manifestations of emotions. Dr. Giniaux observes in his book (op. cit.) that when two horses want to befriend each other in a pasture, they nip at each other in this area.

d) The fifth cervical vertebra, as it seems that there is a secret affinity between this vertebra and the first lumbar. Once, a human chiropractor who was attending one of my clinics asked me if there was, with the horse as with the human, a "symmetry" of symptoms between the vertebrae (if your neck hurts, very often the chiropractor will take care of your pelvis, and vice versa). I must say I didn't know, but I set out investigating the problem, and sure enough, I found some examples of a possible symmetry around the eighth thoracic vertebra. The first cervical is certainly linked with the last two lumbar vertebrae (sixth and fifth seem to act like one; Barbs and Arabians have only five lumbar vertebrae). And the first thoracic seems linked to the 15th thoracic (emotions; remember the horse who sweats abnormally).

Once, this FEI rider on her Grand Prix horse told me that she could not put her hand behind the saddle, because the horse would buck. I palpated; the first lumbar seemed sore. Before she dismounted, I went to the front part of the horse, took care of a blocking at C5, and lo and behold, the sensitivity behind the saddle was gone!

e) The first cervical vertebra. For that, I have no explanation.

This is so much so that castration problems can predispose a horse to develop a whole series of vertebral blockings. It starts with L1 (L stands for lumbar), which is linked to the sexual organs, and then jumps to C5 (C stands for cervical) by reason of this "symmetry" I have established, and from there to wherever, T1 more than likely (T stands for thoracic). Etc...

All the same, endocrine problems will predispose a horse (and more so a mare) to vertebral blockings. This because the connection "vertebra/organ" is a two-way road. It works from the vertebra to the organ, but it also works from the organ to the vertebra (one more time, refer to Giniaux's book).

One time the owner of a two year old cryptorchid stallion asked me if I could help. I answered, "Perhaps," since I knew that Dr. Giniaux, working the right points by acupressure and releasing the tension in L1, would help horses in this case in descending their testicles.

It so happened that the young horse we are talking about was displaying a whole series of vertebral blockings *in his neck!* Now, that horse had never had a saddle on his back or a bit in his mouth. He was fresh from the pasture; nobody had ever pulled on his mouth.

I called Dr. Giniaux to ask him whether he had observed the same thing with young stallions. He said, "No, but I have seen this happen with young fillies with hormonal problems." A possible explanation of this phenomenon could lie in this secret affinity I have mentioned between L1 and C5.

This new science, coupled with equine acupuncture, opens exhilarating new perspectives. We are on the verge of understanding our horses better, and helping them better. Perhaps some readers will think I am a little "off the wall," but if you believe in acupuncture, you probably know that a scar, situated on the course of a meridian, may alter the flow of energy in this meridian. Now imagine a scar on

"Wei Shu," the command point of the stomach meridian. The flow of energy in this meridian will be altered. The horse will develop stomach problems, and guess what? His 12th thoracic vertebra will tend to be blocked!

You will tell me that I am venturing into a realm which is not mine, to wit: medicine. Correct. But it so happens that T12 is right under the saddle, and as a rider, I am most concerned with blockings in this area.

Most veterinarians are not aware of the pathology of the vertebrae; some are still non-believers. It will take much time before all this is taught in the veterinary schools. It will take much time before the average veterinarian knows about all this, and when they know, they won't have enough time to dwell on a horse's vertebral "pattern," because a colicking horse is waiting for their help, because this broodmare is about to foal, etc...

Plus, they will only take care of the obvious, the big cases, the really ailing horses. But what if my horse has a problem of flying change that proceeds from some discomfort created by a vertebral lesion? Sorry, I can't be indifferent. As a trainer, it's my business to palpate, find the lesion, and take care of it if I can. If my horse is lame because he has a rock in his foot, I won't call the vet; I will pull out the rock, and this is not illegal exercise of medicine.

Back to our subject.

• What about emotional horses, worriers, etc? You will always find them with a blocking of the atlas and a blocking of T1. These blockings may be the source of their problems. For instance, a blocked atlas will slow the blood flow to the brain. The brain will be under-oxygenated, the horse will develop headaches, his vision will be impaired, he will spook, rear, etc...

But as I have said, the process is reversible. A worrier, time and again, will block his atlas, and possibly his first thoracic. Dr. Giniaux told me once that he has a friend who suffers from terrible headaches. It so happens that his atlas was blocked, which Dr. Giniaux took care of. The migraines went away...for a while. Ten days later, the gentleman was back at Dr. Giniaux's with an atlas problem and a head-splitting migraine. The migraine was not the consequence but the cause of the atlas being blocked. It would be interesting to ask human chiropractors whether they observe an increase in cases of subluxation of the atlas in their clients around the 15th of April.

The same applies to horses. There is in Texas a mare who could not be ridden for seven years, because of her temper tantrums. She would all of a sudden spin, and bolt, and rear, and dispose of her rider. And she was unpredictable.

We found out that she was suffering from a strong blocking of the third thoracic vertebra, which probably, depending on the direction the rider's weight was bearing on her, created a sudden unbearable pain. We took care of this problem (and of a few others, probably accruing to this one), and she could again be ridden.

As she was progressing satisfactorily, her owner asked me to start working her in hand, against the wall, in order to foster "mobility in place." The mare collected spectacularly, and as she was full of impulsion, among the applause from the audience, instead of mobility in place, she started a soft passage that I accepted wholeheartedly.

Then I let her rest for a few minutes and took on trying again; but this time, it didn't work at all, the mare looked furious, and she would try to "force" my hand forward. I understood that something was wrong. Just in case, almost mechanically, I checked her T3; it had become blocked again! And this was a direct result of the emotion she had experienced, perhaps because of the applause. (Dr. Giniaux tells me that for the human, emotions translate into a blocking of T4.)

Here again, working in hand, when a horse tries to force the rider's hand, one can rig him with sidereins and "animate" him actively with the whip; but every bit of the horse's spinal column will become blocked, and we will produce only one of those miserable shufflings which too often bear the name *piaffe*. And a sad horse, to boot.

• Horses catching their hip in the door post. In the past, I would worry only if there was a big cut in the skin. But for the rest, I thought that this was a minor incident. I know better now. It does not take much force, in some cases, to reset a horse's pelvis. Conversely, it does not take much to offset it. The pelvis is linked to the sacrum, which is comprised of five fused vertebrae and a triangular bone pointing rearward. All this is pretty much rigid. The two sensitive points are: on the one hand the sacroiliac joints, which very often happen to be in a state of "subluxation"; and on the other hand the sacro-lumbar joint, between the sixth lumbar and the first sacral. A blocking of the sixth lumbar can, in time, have dire consequences. Firstly, the horse will quit urinating properly, the act of "micturition" having become painful; he will discharge his bladder only when he cannot resist anymore. This will entail a local poisoning by urea. The horse's coat will lose its shine. Secondly, the atlas (1st cervical) will be blocked, with all the bad behavioral consequences we know.

So, a horse's catching his hip in the door post is not, definitely not, a negligible incident.

The same could be stated about a horse panicking in the cross ties. Here, the process works the other way around; the primal lesion appears in the atlas, but the backward repercussions may be the same, more so, of course, if the horse has fallen on his butt.

• Let's speak of horses who are taught how to "bow," one front leg forward and the other backward. I once applied my "flexion-relaxation" technique to a mare in San Antonio, TX, who happened to be a good inch higher in her left hip than in her right hip. At that time, I was proceeding from rear to front. No flexion of the rear end had evened up that mare's pelvis; it was only when I arrived at the level of T1, which she had quite much blocked, that things came back into order.

Upon that, the owner of the mare, who wanted to show off, asked the mare to "bow." She did it nicely, and lo and behold, when she stood back up, we were back to square one, her left hip was one inch higher than her right hip. The owner was shocked. "Do you think it's the bow?" he said. "What else," I answered. "So, no more bow?" "No more bow!"

[48]

Asking a horse to "bow" amounts to straining his shoulders. A horse is not built for that movement.

• Saddle fitting. Saddle fitting has become a concern amongst riders, and rightfully so. But they focus only on the division of the weight, trying to make it as uniform as possible, which is laudable. They do not realize, however, that most dressage saddles bear on the horse's shoulders. Look toward the rear upper corner of the shoulder blade; you'll find that most often, it is already engaged at least one inch under the saddle.

Now, when a horse moves one front leg forward, the lower part of the shoulder blade also moves forward, but its upper part moves *backwards*, adding three or four inches to the inch we have mentioned, so much so that the shoulder blade engages four to five inches under the saddle. And most often those big German saddles are quite rigid; they don't give much.

It is my belief that when a horse cannot move his shoulders in the proper direction or with the proper amplitude, because of the constraint brought upon him by the saddle, the vertebrae situated between the shoulder blades, to wit T1, T2, and T3, are at risk of being blocked.

• Side reins, draw reins, etc. are dangerous to the extent that they tend to lower the horse's head while encouraging him to take a strong contact with the bit. Here is why:

There are many reasons why a vertebra gets blocked. One of them is compression of one vertebra against another, a more likely danger for the cervical vertebrae. Everybody is aware of the existence of intervertebral discs, but for many, this is the beginning and the end of their knowledge in that matter. They imagine the discs like rings, "washers" surrounding the spinal cord. Now, this is not so. The discs do not surround the spinal cord; they are situated only on the ventral part of the spinal column.

Unlike the human's or the dog's, which feature a fibrous nucleus, providing them with an oblong section and also some resistance against deformation, the discs of a horse (according to Dr. Giniaux's book) are made of a gelatinous substance enclosed in an envelope. This gelatinous substance is not compressible, but it is deformable, so when the disc is compressed, it "juts out" on both extremities. At the ventral extremity, this does not offer any danger. But on the other extremity, next to the spinal cord, from which the disc is separated only by a thin ligament, there is some chance that the disc will push against the spinal cord. This may be very painful and, at any rate, very dangerous.

To this, nature will react by blocking the vertebra or vertebrae, which prevents further damage but in the meantime perpetuates the problem. A "reflex arc" is created, whereby a stimulus is sent from the endangered area ("Mayday!") to a nervous center and another stimulus sent back ("Hold on!"). And as we know, nature will never send a signal of "End of alarm." Manipulating becomes necessary.

Most often, these blockings in the cervical segment create pain. This pain will radiate through the whole front end, affecting the movement of the front legs. If the blocking settles in at the level of the seventh cervical, the blood flux in the front legs and feet will be impaired. Navicular disease can be the result. Dr. Giniaux was telling me that he once was in charge of the horses of an international jumping rider, who would make use and abuse of the draw reins. Now, he said he has never seen as many cases of navicular disease as with these horses.

Correctly used, that is, if they become loose when the horse has responded to their action, draw reins will not create any compression of the neck; the same with side reins if they are not equipped with an elastic "doughnut." To be honest, I must recognize that Plintzner, who wrote the last part of Steinbrecht's book **The Gymnasium of the Horse,** already stated that any "tie down," in order to be efficient, should be loose, i.e., that a horse should never lean on them. What puzzles me is why he does not extend this logic to the reins in general.

The elastic doughnuts work wonders in the beginning, because they deceive the horse, who cannot lean on them. But the particularity of an elastic doughnut being that it never really "gives," since it always pulls back, a horse is never rewarded when he yields, and this will rapidly induce him to try the other solution, i.e., to pull and establish a strong contact as a precaution against the "boomerang effect" of the doughnut.

This is perhaps what the users of that kind of device are looking for: a horse that lowers his head and looks constantly for contact. Now, this will compress the vertebrae of the neck.

The reasoning is simple. To establish a contact, the horse has to move his mouth away from the rider's hand; he can do that only by contracting the muscles of the neck situated above the spinal column. But to lower the head, the horse must contract the muscles of the neck situated under the spinal column. So both the muscles situated above and beneath the cervical vertebral segment will work in contraction, which can only result in compressing the vertebrae against each other.

We have now entered the realm of riding as such, and this leads me to examine now the riding process in the light of the discoveries of Dr. Giniaux.

Conventional equestrian wisdom in the light of osteopathy

A) Work on a circle, bending a horse

The law I dubbed "tridimensional" states that if one bends a horse, all the convex segments of his spinal column are going to undergo an outward rotation. Now with the exception of a short segment going from C6 to T2, the whole of the spinal column of a horse is convex, which means that bending a horse to the right will foster a rotation of the spinous processes to the left and vice versa.

This will tend to lift the inside hip, and not to lower it, as was believed until now. The result is that on a circle, the outside hock will be loaded, not the inside hock as Steinbrecht holds in his **The Gymnasium of the Horse** (Xenophon Press). This is also true for a shoulder-in, and it belies La Guérinière himself, though the founder of this movement.

By working the shoulder-in, La Guérinière wanted to work one side at a time, one hock at a time. This still holds true, although he did not correctly assess which side it was about.

In all the bent movements, conventional wisdom prescribes that the rider's weight be placed inside, and this is confirmed by the "tridimensional" law. Supposing that the rider places his/her weight to the right, the right lateral will be overloaded. To even up the weight borne by each of his laterals, the horse is likely to rotate his rib cage to the left, bringing the rider's weight back at the mid-distance of each lateral. Now, this rotation is welcome, since it is an outward rotation, which can only help the horse in bending laterally and in increasing the natural convexity of his back (collection).

[52]

Nuno Oliveira prescribes bringing the weight to the outside in a shoulder-in. This does not fit the purpose of bending. Yet he may have wanted to increase, in this way, the burden of the outside hock, already loaded by the effect of the bending, in order to make it flex more (but this is questionable, since the reaction of a horse can then be to "arm" himself against the strain).

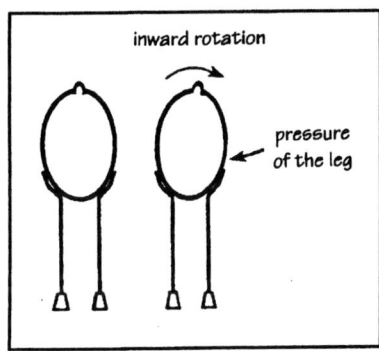

Fig.8 - Rib cage inward rotation upon spur pressure.

Conventional wisdom also prescribes using the inside leg at the girth in order to foster bending. Given the disproportion existing between the strength of a human's leg and the stiffness of a horse's rib cage, there is very little chance that this procedure will work. But if one tries to bolster the effect of the leg by using the spur, then we are one hundred percent wrong, since the action of the spur, assuming that the horse yields to it, would tend to push away, outwardly, the bottom of the rib cage, entailing by the same token an inward rotation of the spinal column, which can only foster concavity, that is, flattening of the back and loss of engagement (see Fig. 8).

So to bend a horse, one should limit oneself to using the inside indirect rein (which does not prevent the croup from moving inwards, whereas the direct rein does) and settling one's weight inwardly.

B) Lateral movements

Conventional wisdom stresses the utility of lateral movements: shoulder-in, haunches-in, half pass. Now, they should be dealt with with extreme prudence and progressiveness, lest they be dangerous for the horse's structural integrity.

In a half pass, the crossing over of the outside shoulder over the inside shoulder tends to foster an inward rotation of the withers, hence of the spinal column. Yet this rotation is opposed by the lateral bending of the horse, which tends to create an outward rotation of the spinal column. So somewhere along the spinal column, a "torque" will be created, which can only foster vertebral blockings. Experience shows that the level affected by this torque is that of the first thoracic vertebra.

One of the flexions to do in order to release a blocking at this level consists of bending the horse's neck to the side of the blocking as one makes the horse cross his outside front leg over his inside front leg. Now, this is nothing else than an amplification of the gesture of a half pass.

I have mentioned the "homeopathic" character of the osteopathic manipulation ("like treats like"). This entails that the gesture, for the flexion, should reproduce and slightly exaggerate the gesture which in the first place could have created the problem.

One therefore has here the demonstration of the possible harmful effect of a half pass.

I once discovered that by setting a horse with, for instance, his right front leg forward and then bending the neck to the right, one could release vertebral blockings situated to the right side of the neck. This frightened me, because if the healing gesture has to imitate the harmful gesture (and slightly overdo it), something as simple as turning a horse's head as he moves one leg forward could be danger- ous. Better quit riding, if this were true.

I called Dr. Giniaux, and his answer was: "It is not the gesture in itself, i.e., in this case, the bending of the neck combined with the stretching of one front leg, which is dangerous. This will only predispose the horse to get these blockings. But if then there is a stress, because the horse is afraid, or because of an emotion, or because the movement was forced upon him, then the lesions will settle in. It is the stress which is the determining factor."

Coming back to our half pass, one has to understand that it is not the half pass in itself which is dangerous; it would be the fact of imposing it upon the horse, of forcing him. So not only should we be very progressive in our demands, but we also should work in a calm and reassuring environment. This has been said time and again in the past, but it is now confirmed by the osteopath.

It came as a surprise to me when I realized that shoulder-in could also be dangerous. This flies in the face of all the classical principles. And yet...

I am speaking here of the "classical" shoulder-in, that of La Guérinière, in which four tracks are traced on the ground, and in which the inside hind leg crosses slightly over the outside hind leg, bringing the inside hind foot into the alignment of the outside hind foot. Since, due to the bending, the horse's inside hip is kept slightly higher than his outside hip, this crossing gesture, however limited, renders still more difficult for the horse the task of setting down his inside foot. The good horse will react to that by bending his outside hock, which is one purpose of the exercise. But a horse with straight or stiff hocks, like, for instance, an Arabian, will cope with the difficulty by rotating his croup inwards, a rotation which clashes with the outward rotation created by the lateral bending.

The torque here will more than likely harm the lumbar vertebrae, or T18, the last thoracic vertebra, situated at the junction between a rather "stiff" segment (the thoracic segment, which is linked to eighteen pairs of ribs), and a more supple segment, the lumbar segment.

So shoulder-in is a double-edged sword. If it succeeds, it does much good. If it fails, it can be harmful. Therefore Steinbrecht's advice to start this exercise with a small angle seems perfectly justified.

On the other hand, the exercise as practiced nowadays by the German school, in which the haunches remain practically perpendicular to the direction of movement, does not offer the same risks. Yet, except for the muscular advantages that can result from the crossing over of the front legs, it doesn't avail much benefit, since it does not set the horse on the haunches. But it is probably a good thing to start with this type of shoulder-in and finish with the authentic one, that of La Guérinière.

C) Rider's position on a circle

Conventional wisdom has it that on a circle the rider's shoulders should remain parallel to the horse's, and that the rider's haunches should remain parallel to the horse's. In other words, his/her shoulders should rotate inwards as his/her haunches rotate outward. This proceeds from the opinion that when a horse is bent, his haunches remain perpendicular to his spinal column (hence on a radius to the circle), which is true, and that the shoulders also remain perpendicular to the spinal column, which is wrong.

When a horse is bent to the right, for instance, he will try to alleviate the constraint brought upon his right side by forwarding his right shoulder, which he can do, due to the absence of a collar bone in the equine. Moreover, the shape of his rib cage in its front part is tapering off, which is one more facilitating feature. In addition, the bending will have fostered an outward rotation of the spinal column, which lifts the inside, here the right shoulder. For all these reasons, when a horse is bent, his inside shoulder moves forward. This is why, incidentally, a correctly bent horse will canter with the inside fore leading.

Besides, the great Masters of the past, like La Guérinière and d'Aure, had already noticed that when on a circle, a horse forwards his inside shoulder (Fig. 9).

Surprisingly, this does not belie the principle that the rider's shoulders should remain parallel to the horse's. But to do that they have to rotate outward and not inwards. Therefore to adapt his/her posture to that of the horse, the rider will have to rotate both his/her haunches and shoulders outward. This implies that he/she will lengthen the outside rein appropriately, since if he/she would content

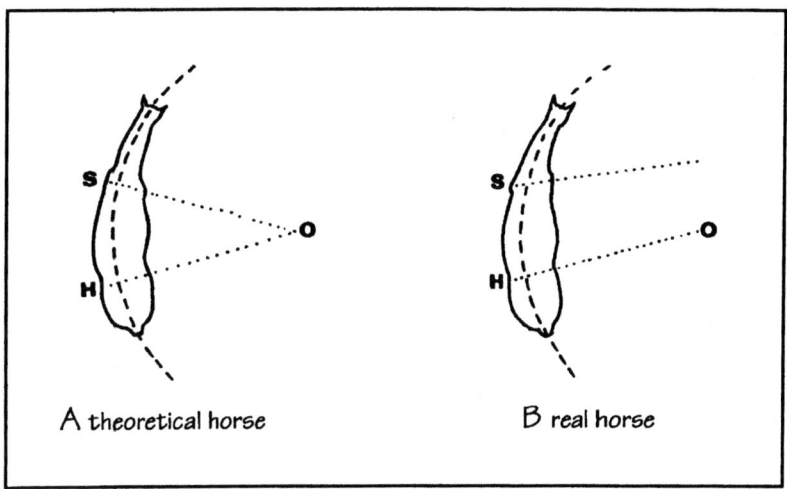

Fig. 9 - Respective directions of haunches and shoulders.
A = In theory. B= In practice.

him/herself with moving the outside hand forward, this movement
would oppose the necessary backing of the outside shoulder.

D) Lowering of the haunches

Conventional equestrian wisdom has it that when collected, a
horse should lower his haunches. This is a correct statement, because
collection corresponds to a state of arousal of the horse's alertness;
the horse wants to be ready for action, he wants to be able to leap
forward if need be, and for this, he will slightly bend his hocks. This
bending, in turn, lowers the haunches.

This visual impression of lowering of the haunches will also be
increased by the elevation of the withers resulting from the lifting of
the rib case between the shoulders.

But this is about it. Too pronounced a lowering of the haunches
is not a proof of excellence; it is a strong indication that the horse is
blocked in his front end.

Steinbrecht has enunciated the theory of the two arm lever, which
holds that by lifting a horse's head, one lowers his haunches. He
thinks that the horse's vertebral column will hinge around the

[57]

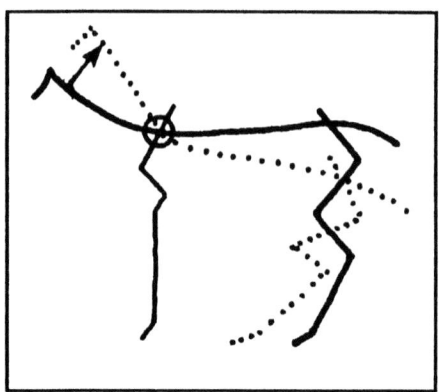

Fig. 10 - Theory of the two arm lever according to Steinbrecht, as described by Gen. Decarpentry in Academic Equitation, page 72 (J.A. Allen & Co. Ltd., Publishers, London).

shoulders, so that when one segment of the "lever" rises, the other sinks Fig. 10).

But General Decarpentry does not agree: he (rightfully) denies the existence of a pivot for the spinal column around the shoulders, for, he says, horses have no collar bone. But he states (erroneously) that lifting the head will automatically result in collapsing the withers.

What happens really, as we have seen, is that when the neck is lifted, so are the withers. This movement generally entails a slanting of the pelvis, that is, an engagement of the hindquarter, through the flexion of the sacro-lumbar joint, more so if the horse is set in motion; however, this engagement of the hindquarter may or may not (Fig. 11) be accompanied with a "lowering" of the haunches properly speaking, that is, a flexion of the three main joints in the rear end, to wit "hip joint" (coxo-femoral joint), stifle, and hock. Only in perfect collection will all those joints be flexed simultaneously, combining the tilting of the pelvis with the lowering of the haunches (more on this subject in Appendix 3).

Yet it is probably possible to partially justify Steinbrecht's observation, if not theory. Horses who are blocked in their cervical or first thoracic vertebrae cannot lift their withers. Hence is the "fixed point," the "pivot" observed by Steinbrecht, brought into existence.

Due to the strong effects of reins in German riding, the seeking for a permanent contact with the rider's hand, even in a piaffe, which is likely to compress the cervical vertebrae, such horses must have been galore at the time of Steinbrecht. Needless to say, the bending

Fig. 11 - Elevation of the neck and withers create engagement of hind-quarters (tilting of pelvis) but, in this case, no lowering of haunches.

of the hocks accruing from the elevation of the neck in their case becomes strained and painful. It is more a crushing of the rear end than a healthy flexion.

My personal observation has shown me that when, working in hand, a horse excessively lowers his rear end as he flattens his back, it is always an indication that he is blocked in his front.

Baucherism in the light of osteopathy

According to Dr. Giniaux, attempts have been made by some, in France I suppose, to devise a series of "blind" manipulations and flexions that would eliminate through a kind of crosscheck all the existing vertebral lesions, irrespective of their setting and nature. This, of course, is impossible, because, applied blindly, some of those flexions could worsen some already existing lesions, and therefore perhaps start off some others.

And yet it appears that the Baucherist flexions of the neck may partially justify this contention.

Dr. Giniaux's manipulations comprise two stages. In the first, the horse is bent progressively, tactfully, but as much as he can afford. The possibilities of bending are so to say "saturated." Then comes the second stage, which consists of a skillful "push," or "jolt," which will make the horse startle and release the spasm. Without the bending, the "jolt" would not work, but without the "jolt," the bending would have no effect.

Now, I have found out that, as concerns the cervical segment, and even the very beginning of the thoracic segment, and upon the horse's neck being properly bent, *the yielding of the jaw has the same effect as a jolt.*

As concerns the bending, the tri-dimensional law I have mentioned shows that, for a blocking of "concave" nature, it should be done on the side of the blocking (to create more inward rotation); and the ears should not tip outward but inwards if possible, or at least remain in a horizontal line, which is also a requirement of the Baucherist flexions of the neck.

Therefore it is shown that the flexions of Baucher may constitute osteopathic manipulations. In fact, they do release blockings of the cervical vertebrae, when those blockings are not too rebellious. I shall come back to this observation when I deal more in depth with the "flexion-relaxations."

What characterizes Baucher is his extraordinary power of intuition. Baucher "felt" things that the ordinary rider cannot or at least does not feel. A certain feel is required to assess when a vertebra has yielded. This feel is exactly the same as the feel required for getting the yielding of the jaw. This tact, Baucher could not communicate through a book. He believed that he was fighting the stiffness of muscles, whereas it seems now that he was fighting vertebral blockings. But the explanation of the phenomenon, the justification of the technique, matters less than the result.

This is why all that has been said on the necessity of cultivating "firm" necks, the allegations that Baucher would eventually create "weak" or "depressed" necks, all this is preposterous. A "firm" neck is nothing else than a neck hosting vertebral blockings. When rid of these blockings, a horse's neck is not "weak" or "soft"; it is free.

And yes, by multiplying these flexions (completed with a jaw flexion, let's not forget), to the right and to the left, and at different levels of the neck, for several days in a row to start with, and then only in case of unexpected difficulties (probably new blockings settling in), Baucher would sort of "crosscheck" the process and progressively "rid," "wash" the horse's neck and cranial (front) part of the chest of vertebral blockings.

This "crosschecking" was rendered possible by the fact that the neck flexions, assorted with the jaw flexion, can in no way worsen an already existing lesion. Although they are "blind," they either take care of the problems or are ineffective.

I have also observed that the rotation of the haunches around the shoulders, when correctly done, that is to say when the horse is kept as straight as possible, may release some vertebral blockings in the lumbar area, due to the rotation of the pelvis involved in the exercise.

[61]

If it so happens that, accidentally so to say, the rotation is done in the right direction, it can release a blocking. If it is not done in the right direction, it can be detrimental, "forcing" on a lesion. But in this case, the horse will not freely lend himself to the exercise; the depth of his engagement and crossing movement will be limited by the lesion, and here comes the "tact." If, in spite of the reluctance of the horse, the trainer tries to "force" him into the movement, harm will be done.

The "Géricault Case"

To start, for those not familiar with my book **Racinet explains Baucher**, let me quote from it a few lines dealing with Baucher's training a young, difficult Thoroughbred, named 'Géricault':

"...1842 is the year when Baucher's prowess with 'Géricault' took place. 'Géricault' was a three year old Thoroughbred stallion who was bucking all his riders off. His owner, the Englishman Lord Seymour, had let it be known that he would give the horse to anyone who could, without falling, tour on his back the 'Bois de Boulogne,' a park near Paris. A representative of the 'anti-Baucherist' camp, Vicomte de Tournon had tried and failed. Comte de Lancosme-Bresves, a recent convert to Baucher, had succeeded, albeit by a trick, since he had had himself surrounded by a group of friends on horseback during the whole trip, so closely that 'Géricault' hadn't had much chance to fight.

"But right or wrong, he had won the bet and Lord Seymour gave him the horse, which he in turn gave to Baucher, as an homage. Whereupon Baucher declared that he would show 'Géricault' at the circus *within a month.*

"27 days later, in the light of the gas chandeliers, amid the brouhaha of the crowd and the hubbub of the band, a calm and disciplined 'Géricault' performed a program which included lateral work, canter pirouettes, single flying changes of lead, and a magnificent, slow, majestic rein back by which he went out of the ring."

Baron d'Etreillis wrote: "After having brilliantly contributed to his master's glory, 'Géricault' was sold to Mr. de Moncoussin, *an average rider*, who used him for several years, with everyone in Paris' knowledge."

I will certainly not tarnish Baucher's merit by trying to find an osteopathic explanation for this feat.

1842 was the year Baucher published his **Method of equitation based on new principle**. His first "manner" was in full bloom. The flexions he was practicing at that time were quite extensive. One of them consisted of having the horse literally look toward his behind before a jaw flexion was asked for.

I have found out that this flexion may release a blocking at the level of the third thoracic vertebra. It is not the best way to get this release, but anyway it works.

Also, it so happens that, as I have already mentioned in this book, horses whose third thoracic vertebra is blocked may have very violent, uncontrollable reactions, due to a sudden pain, depending on the direction the rider's weight was applying on the back.

So it may well be (we will never know) that this is exactly what "Géricault" was suffering from. The manipulations — sorry, flexions — done by Baucher having taken care of the pain, "Géricault" became what most horses basically are: a good boy.

This does not diminish the stature of Baucher, because it's still a feat to take a young, totally untrained horse and show him one month later at a circus in already rather sophisticated movements such as canter pirouettes and flying changes.

It is my belief that if "Géricault" had been suffering from painful blockings located from T13, for instance, to T16, that is, under the saddle, Baucher would have lost his bet, because "Géricault" would have "fought," or rather reacted strongly (he would have fought the pain, not the rider).

Supposing even that the powerful means of domination used by Baucher would have allowed him to make "Géricault" perform in spite of the pain (but can a horse do a canter pirouette if his back hurts, even when the rider's name is Baucher?), the horse could not have been sold to Mr. de Moncoussin, "an average rider." Obviously, what Mr. de Moncoussin had bought was a pacified, happy horse.

What I am trying to say is that there are no horses who fight without a reason. In 99 percent of the cases, the reason is physical. "Géricault" was not a "fighting horse" who had been "tamed" by Baucher in such a way that he had acquired such a fear of the human that he was subdued forever; this is cowboy reasoning.

As I have mentioned here above, the rotations of the haunches around the shoulders may also have helped rid the horse of vertebral blockings in the lumbar area. I have also said that they require tact to prevent them from being harmful, but tact was not a problem for Baucher. A "locking" of L6, for instance, brings difficulties at a canter: the horse will always keep the same hind leg leading and will cross-canter when asked to perform on the other side. This blocking can also provoke a kind of "bucking" when cantering, but not the kind of bucking likely to "unhook" the rider.

Another aspect of the question is, when L6 is blocked, so will the "atlas" be, and the "mise en main" ("bringing in hand") will become difficult if not impossible.

So much so that the whole "arsenal" of Baucher's flexions, added to his tact and capacity of observation, may have transformed a previously crippled horse into a sound and happy one.

Also, it probably so happened that the "healing" virtue of his flexions coincided with the pathological "pattern" of the horse. This is sheer luck.

But luck is also part of the lot of great men. When somebody was proposing an officer for promotion to Napoleon, he would regularly ask, "Does he have good luck?"

Flexion - Relaxations

To perform these flexions, the horse must be mouthed with a full cheek snaffle bit. The reins are left on the horse's neck. Braided reins or rubber reins should be avoided, coarse reins being an obstacle to the necessary "feel."

A) Atlas

The atlas is the first cervical vertebra. It is situated next to the skull (occiput). Its length is about three to four inches, depending on the horse's size. Its lateral processes are shaped like "wings," and it is the edge of these wings that one can feel, right behind the jowls. Severe blockings of the atlas may be very harmful, due to the restriction of the blood flow in the brain they bring about, occasioning headaches, vision troubles, and behavioral problems (shying and rearing). (Cf. Dr. Giniaux, op. cit.)

But many horses who do not present these extreme symptoms are nevertheless afflicted with minor blockings of the "atlanto-occipital" joint that can noticeably impair their performances.

Although strong blockings of the atlas should be left to the care of an equine chiropractor or an equine osteopath, these minor blockings have to be addressed and are amenable to "flexion-relaxations."

Evaluation: Position yourself to the left side of the horse, facing his left jowl. Set your right hand against the atlas and, as you softly resist with this hand, pull the horse's head to the left, using the rein or the side piece of the headstall (Fig. 12). The horse's head should

Fig. 12 - Positioning for palpation of C1 (atlas).

Fig. 13 - Atlanto-occipital joint free (to the left).

Fig. 14 - Atlanto-occipital joint blocked (to the left).

Fig. 15 - Unlocking atlanto-occipital joint, first flexion.

Fig. 16 - Unlocking atlanto-occipital joint, the right side.

yield and rotate somewhat as if "unscrewing" from the neck, and in the meantime turn somewhat to the left (Fig. 13).

If this does not happen, or worse, if the horse fights (Fig. 14), the joint between occiput and atlas is blocked. Palpate in the same way on the other side. Usually, the blocking on the right side is stronger than the blocking on the left side.

Flexion - relaxation: Face the horse, lift his head to a maximum, the bit pushing onto the upper jaw (Fig. 15). Resist in this position until you feel some relief with the horse. Immediately drop the reins. The head falls in a vertical position or thereabout. Most often, the blocking will have disappeared on the left side (fig. 13).

For the right side, face the horse, lift his head, and make it tilt to the left, the right ear being higher than the left ear (Fig. 16). Resist both softly and firmly, until you feel the relief. The head should turn to the right (your left) when the blocking gives in.

B) Axis

The axis is the second thoracic vertebra. Its blocking, as well as that of the third cervical vertebra, is likely to bring about mouth problems (difficult relationship with the bit, mastication problems, teeth problems, etc.). (Cf. Giniaux.)

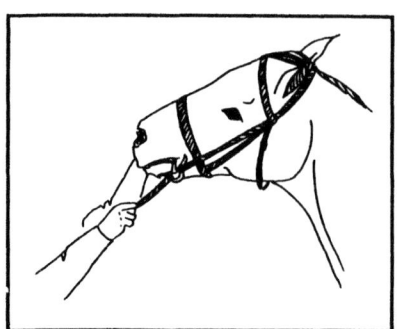

Evaluation: Palpation of this vertebra requires some training. Palpate with the outside edge of the hand. This vertebra is in a semi-vertical position. It does not protrude as much as the first and third cervical vertebrae. Its mobility is very easy to feel, and so is its blocking.

Fig. 17 -Flexion-relaxation for second cervical, when blocked to the left; works as well for second thoracic.

Flexion - relaxation: The same as the flexion described for the left side of the atlas. But, of course, translate to the side you are working (Fig. 17).

With all the cervical vertebrae, it may happen that as you release one side, the other gets blocked, and vice versa, so these flexion-relaxations have to be repeated as many times as needed, the end result being that the vertebrae yield on both sides.

C) From C3 to C7

Evaluation: Classical palpation. You have to push laterally, "through" the neck. Mobility is unmistakable, and so is blocking. If you aren't sure, there is blocking.

Flexion - relaxation: Two types of flexion-relaxations may be applied, depending on the results. The first type is the flexion described for C1 left side and for C2. Try to position yourself right in the axis of the horse, or in such a way that the neck is kept straight, since the flexion starts with a "torsion" of the neck. But as soon as the blocking gives in, on the contrary, accompany the horse as he turns his head inside. When you drop the reins, the head should stay in the bent position for a short while of its own accord. If the head

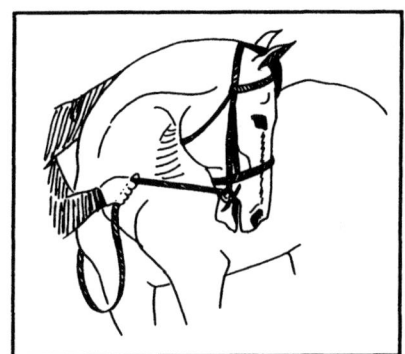

Fig. 18 - Lateral flexion à la
Baucher.

immediately comes back into the alignment of the body, more than likely the flexion didn't work.

Knowing when to resist and when to yield belongs to the domain of art. Words can only explain so much. Do not apply a flexion-relaxation mechanically; try to be "with the horse." Concentrate your mind on the level you are dealing with (most important).

The second type of flexion relaxation: the flexion "à la Baucher." Bend the neck laterally at the targeted level, maintain the line of the ears in the horizontal, and get a flexion of the jaw; the blocking should yield when the jaw yields. Apply your authority in a calm and firm manner; never fight, don't use force. Wait calmly for the result to happen. Don't be demanding (Fig. 18).

The more you go down the line of the cervical vertebrae, the more the flexion "à la Baucher" works. C7 and more so T1 yield very well with this type of flexion.

In all the flexions "à la Baucher," if the yielding of the jaw lingers, it can be good to provoke it by pushing the bit (without altering the bending) up onto the upper jaw, which opens the angle at the poll but provokes the desired jaw yielding.

Time and again, come back to the levels you have previously released; they may be blocked again, as if the blocking was wandering.

Never get angry. Remember that stress is the triggering factor for all blockings.

There is a very interesting flexion-relaxation which may work for all the blockings situated in the area of the neck; it consists of moving the horse's front leg forward on the side of the blockings, in the meantime bending his neck on the same side. The horse's weight should rest on the outside foreleg, the leg which is not stretched. To make sure that this happens, observe the stretched foreleg as you progressively bend the horse, and see to it that this leg "wobbles" more or less, showing that its weight does not rest on the ground. If and when the horse moves his foreleg back, drop the outside rein and increase the inside bending. This flexion may release several blockings in one stroke.

Particular case of C6: When a flexion "à la Baucher" does not work, have somebody lift the horse's head (fore and aft) as you subsequently pull onto the withers, toward the blocked side.

D) T1, T2, T3

Evaluation: These vertebrae are situated between the shoulders, which renders their palpation very difficult, if not impossible. While the vertical spinous process of T1 cannot be felt, any blockings of T1's vertebral body is easy to feel by pushing your fist right against the edge of the scapulum (shoulder blade). The top of the third thoracic may be felt in front of the withers, under the cord of the nuchal ligament. This requires experience, but you will never acquire this experience if you don't try. The second thoracic cannot be felt, but its blocking always brings about a kind of swelling and, at any rate, a tension in the area of the neck in front of the scapulum, at the level of the upper third of this scapulum.

By the end of a session of flexion-relaxations, when everything seems in good order, and as you are about to let the horse go "home," check the second thoracic vertebra; very often, it's blocked, as if it were a last refuge for the resistances. In this latter case, the blocking yields to the slightest solicitation.

As I have already mentioned, blockings of T3 may be very painful, leading a horse to swerve dangerously, rear, etc. They also tend to narrow the track of the front feet, sometimes drastically.

T3 is not very mobile by itself. Nevertheless, the blocking of this vertebra is not difficult to diagnose.

Flexion - relaxation: T1 is usually very easy to release, through a flexion "à la Baucher." The bending should start immediately in front of the shoulder blade. Keep the head vertical (ears on a horizontal line), *but not at any cost* (Fig. 18).

In the case of a T1 that you cannot liberate with this flexion, make the horse cross his front leg opposite to the side of blocking, over the front leg on the side of the blocking. As you keep this leg in this position, bend the neck on the side of the blocking. This is nothing else than the exaggeration of the gesture of the horse's front end in a half pass.

You should not fight, more so the person who keeps the front leg crossed. Very often, it is when the release happens that the horse tries to liberate himself from the constraint. Accept it. Just go with the horse.

T2 yields to the flexion by torsion already described for the cervical. Lift the horse's head, but not excessively. Keep the angle of the poll as open as possible. Accompany the movement of the head when it turns inwards, indicating that the blocking has yielded, but don't let the head go down in this bending movement. You should feel that the head is light and does not bear on your hands.

There are two flexion - relaxations for T3.

For the first, bend the horse (with reins over the neck), on the side of the blocking, and with the other hand, at the level of the chest and with one finger, try to spot the interval between the first and second rib, next to the sternum on the side of the blocking (Fig. 19). Press this point; very often, you will feel a yielding in the tension at this level, and T3 will have yielded by the same token. Although all this feel is very subtle, it is also unmistakable.

In case of a rebellious blocking of T3, take the front leg on the side of the blocking and cross it over the front leg on the side opposite to the blocking. Maintain this leg in this crossed over position and progressively bend the horse's head on the side of the blocking. This is nothing else than the exaggeration of the gesture of the horse's front end in a shoulder-in.

[73]

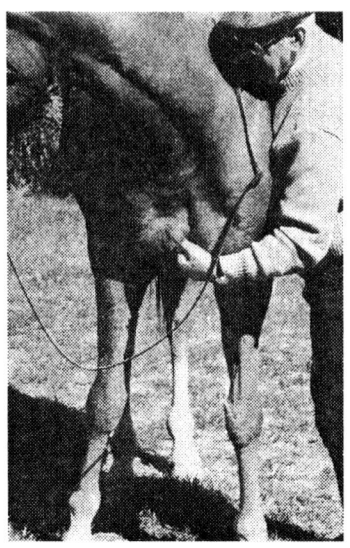
Fig. 19 - Flexion-relaxation for T3

Same recommendations as for T1: don't force, ever. Resist if necessary, but with tact. Most often, when the horse tries to "liberate" himself from your grip, the vertebral blocking has yielded.

E) T4 to T10

These are the vertebrae of the withers. Their freedom is utterly necessary to the "fluidity" of a horse's vertebral column. The withers are made of the spinal processes of these vertebrae, which are very long, so whereas the withers are the highest point of a horse's back, the vertebrae, that is, their bodies, lie quite deep inside the horse's torso. The fourth vertebra is the first to be felt on the "crest line" of the withers. The fifth usually marks the top of the withers. The tenth is at the base of the withers, the top of its spinous process is often sharp and easy to identify.

When the withers are "sunken," a lot of pain is involved that could render the horse difficult to ride. At any rate, it will hinder the performance.

Evaluation: These vertebrae must enjoy some lateral mobility. Palpate on both sides and assess this lateral mobility. Don't expect to find a great deal of mobility; nevertheless, the impression should be more or less "mushy." When it's hard, it is really hard and does not yield to the pressure.

Flexion - relaxation: Put one finger against the top of the spinous process on the "mushy" side. Apply some pressure and in the meantime bend the horse's neck, with the rein over the back, as much as it can bend on the side of the blocking. When you feel that the spinous process pushes your finger back toward you, the yielding is completed.

This flexion is difficult to perform because of the strength which is involved in the pressure of your finger when you push the top of the spinous process toward the direction of blocking. This strength impairs one's sensitivity; it tends to clash with the necessary tact.

F) T10 to T18

Evaluation: Difficult, because of the muscles (spinalis and then longissimi dorsi) that can be found on both sides of the vertebral column. They are more prominent just behind the withers. At this level, it is best to try to determine in which way some possible blocking affects the shape of the back.

The presence of the supraspinal ligaments may also interfere with palpating.

Besides, every horse is different.

Flexion - relaxation: The difficulty found in palpating reflects on flexing. The best is to proceed as for the vertebrae of the withers. Only if this happens to be too awkward should one first flex the neck with the reins and only then apply an action on the back. This action should aim at hollowing the back. Most often, the back will respond positively to this "sagittal" flexion, because of the "concave" nature of the blockings. Notice that upon successful completion of the flexion relaxation, it becomes more difficult to hollow the back.

If no result ensues, then you are probably in the presence of a blocking of a "convex" nature, and you should first change the side of the lateral flexion of the neck and then change the direction of the "sagittal" flexion of the body, for instance by applying a hoof pick under the belly at the level one is dealing with.

Applying a hoof pick under the horse's belly is always a good thing, if the horse accepts it, because it may happen that the back, although rising and increasing its convexity, shows a slight "dent," or rather a small alteration of the curvature of the back at the level of the blocking. This in turn would indicate that the nature of the blocking is probably "concave."

G) Lumbar vertebrae

There are six of them, but the Barb and most Arabians have only five.

Evaluation: Very easy, except with the sixth, the last lumbar, which sometimes happens to be fairly "sunken." Because of this particularity, the sixth lumbar is often overlooked. That would be an error, due to the important effects its blocking may have on locomotion (canter). As for any other level, evaluate the lateral mobility of the vertebra and then, by either observing the outline of the horse's back or by evaluating the side of the croup that bends more easily, determine the nature of the blocking, convex or concave.

With race horses, most blockings of the lumbar are "convex," due to their ability to round their backs like greyhounds when they gallop. Therefore "upwards" blockings are much more likely to happen than with the dressage horse.

Flexion - relaxation: At this level, we are far from the front end of the horse, and a neck flexion cannot propagate this far. The lateral flexion should then be obtained by other means.

I give hereunder three ways to influence bending in the rear end:

1) Keep a hind leg back or, on the contrary, engaged under the belly. When one hind leg sets down under the belly, the hip on the same side should be higher (because the lumbar segment is naturally convex) and the croup should be slightly flexed laterally to the same side. If it happens that the hip on this side is lower than the other, then you know that some vertebral blocking or blockings of a "con-

cave" nature keep the lumbar segment tipped to this side. You have to find them.

2) Find a point on the croup (behind the level of the sacro-iliac joint, for instance) which, under pressure, makes the horse "cower" and bend inwards (this does not work if the blockings are of a "concave" nature, because they tend to flatten the back; they oppose its being flexed in a convex manner).

3) Use traction on the tail, to either bend the croup laterally or bend the back in a sagittal plane. Observe attentively, from behind the horse, the general direction of the tail. *If it goes to the left, never pull it to the right, and vice-versa.* That would be forcing the spasm, whatever it is, that keeps the tail in this direction, instead of "deceiving" it, which has constantly been our policy, *in order to do no harm to the horse.*

When you have determined the nature of the spasm, "convex" or "concave," a good method is to use the tail in order to create the lateral flexion, as you would have used the neck for all the other vertebrae, and apply a soft lateral pressure on the "soft" side of the vertebra.

Important remark: If by any chance you had to lift the tail for a back flexion, always check T3 after your flexion, since the lifting of the tail is likely to block T3 again, if it was blocked in the first place. The fragility of the level of T3 probably comes from the fact that it is at a junction between a convex segment and a concave segment.

Some vertebral blockings can also be released through the classic "turn around the shoulders," in hand. I have described the phenomenon in the chapter "Baucherism in the Light of Osteopathy." When you ask for this movement, keep the horse's head high, even if he doesn't like it, and prevent the horse from yielding laterally with his neck (keep him "straight").

H) Pelvis

An important part of a horse's skeleton, it is in the main comprised of the "sacrum" and "ilia." The "sacrum" is a triangular bone, whose point faces rearward, welded to a vertebral segment made of the five fused sacral vertebrae. The "ilia" (plural of "ilium") are two big bones which form the iliac "table," properly speaking. Through the welding of the "pubic symphysis," they form a kind of "ring" encircling the sacrum and positioned at an angle of about thirty degrees with it.

Important luxations of the pelvis are very painful; they result in lameness and should be left to the care of the veterinarian and/or a chiropractor or an equine osteopath.

But the pelvis may also be the setting of minor blockings, which may have some incidence on the locomotion. They can be taken care of by means of flexion-relaxations.

Evaluation: Observing a horse at a walk, his buttocks should move forward and downwards with each step; the croup should oscillate from side to side. These movements should be symmetrical. The swinging movement of the haunches is more pronounced with some horses than with others, but it has to be noticeable. If it does not exist at all, then you know that some serious blocking has settled into the lumbar area or at the joint T18-L1.

Most often, only one side will be blocked. The sacral vertebral segment (right above the tail) moves only to one side. The buttock bone on the side of the blocking is rather immobile; the engagement of the hind leg on this side is only assured by the flexion of the coxo-femoral joint, i.e., the joint between femur and pelvis.

Also: as you push onto the hip, you get a feeling of stony immobility.

Flexion - relaxation: 1) Take the foot by the toe on the blocked side, position it vertically under the hip (not forward from that position), and lift it up strongly, in an absolutely vertical direction, so as to make the horse "hop" on the other hind leg.

2) From behind the horse, carefully observe the direction of the tail (sacral vertebrae). If it goes to the right, the flexion-relaxation will have to be done from the right and vice-versa, irrespective of the side of the blocking. If you cannot make out the direction of the tail, have somebody walk the horse a few steps in front of you.

Then go to the side toward which the tail is oriented, place your elbow against the hip, and as you resist with your elbow, pull the tail toward you.

Check the result, both visually as you walk the horse, and through palpation.

3) Go toward the side opposite to the blocking and palpate the femur at the level of the trochanter. Have somebody walk the horse a few steps as you keep your hand against the trochanter. You will have that feeling of stone numbness. Then push onto the trochanter as the horse walks; you will feel that "something" has yielded.

This, very often, is enough to help the pelvis settle back in the proper position and retrieve its liberty. Again, check the result on the haunch that was blocked.

I) First sacral vertebra

Its junction with the lumbar segment is very important. If it is blocked, the pelvis cannot "tip under," engagement of the hind legs will proceed only from the play of the coxo-femoral joints, and collection will be impossible.

Evaluation: The sacral segment (and it alone) will be "tipped" toward the direction of blocking, entailing a little "dip" in the muscles on this side. Also, there will be some sensitivity in these muscles when you press down with the tip of your fingers.

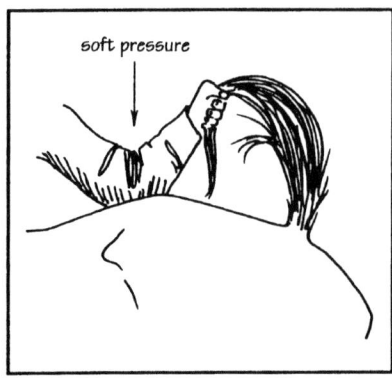

soft pressure

Fig. 20 - Flexion relaxation for S1.

Flexion - relaxation: Take the tail with your right hand if you are on the left side, the left hand if you are on the right side, and set your elbow down next to the first sacral vertebra, perhaps three inches from the middle lineand on the "depressed" side. Lift the tail in a "sagittal" plane as you push down with your elbow (Fig. 20). Don't overdo it.

Remember to check the third thoracic immediately after this flexion.

J) Position of saddle

Before you start working a horse, attentively examine how the

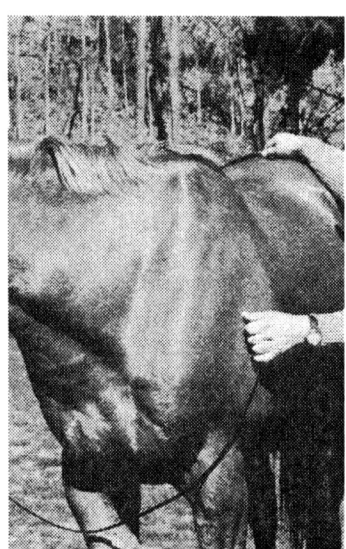

Fig. 21 - Flexion-relaxation while waiting.

saddle rests on his back. If it is in the least "tilted" to one side, the horse has a problem and should not be ridden. You have to palpate in order to find where the problem lies, and this may be time consuming.

In case you are in a hurry or can't succeed in finding the setting of the blocking, you can proceed in this way: assuming that the saddle tilts to the right, for instance, undo the reins at the buckle, place yourself on the left side of the horse, take only the rein on the right side (over the horse's back), and bend the horse calmly, irrespective of the direction the line of his ears will display. Just bend very softly, but to a maximum (Fig. 21). Then wait.

After a while (which can amount to one and a half minute), you will feel a kind of relief with the horse, his back will rise, and the horse will move forward. Let him do so; more than likely, the problem, wherever it was, is solved. Check the new position of the saddle.

This utterly simple technique may also work if you know where the problem lies but you do not want, for whatever reason, to apply your other hand (that which does not hold the active rein) onto the horse's back.

While doing all this, don't let the other rein, the rein you are not holding, drag on the ground. Keep it very loose in your other hand, or ask somebody to hold it by its extremity, without interfering with the flexion.

If you are holding the other rein yourself, the rein on the side opposite to the problem, and in the event the flexion-relaxation is not working after one and a half minutes, you may pull gently and progressively on this rein in order to try to position the line of the horse's ears horizontally (head vertical).

PART THREE

THE SYNTHESIS

Working Posture

lthough I don't much like the notion of "work" in dressage, to which I prefer terms like "schooling," "instruction," "study," etc., I can't resist the pleasure of coining the expression "working posture" as opposed to "working gaits."

Working a horse in his gaits in the hope he will little by little perfect his balance is the long and uncertain method I have mentioned and questioned in this book, adopted by the FEI riders, more or less following the example of the Masters of the pre-Baucherist era.

Working posture (i.e., collection), first as a base for the enhancement of the gaits, is the path of Baucherism.

The fundamental posture, which I have described all along in this book, is created by the engagement of the hindquarters (slanting of pelvis) associated with a lifting of the withers and a flexion at the poll, which remains the highest point of the horse's upper line (Fig. 22).

You will notice that I have described this posture from rear to front, since the slanting of the pelvis is its foundation, the rest being either a condition for or a consequence of this slanting.

Now let's take that description the other way around. It's my belief, and it is confirmed time and again with any horse reasonably devoid of vertebral blockings that the "mise en main" ("bringing in hand") is the necessary and sufficient condition for all the rest to appear, to wit lifting of the withers and engagement of the hindquarters.

"Mise en main" is obtained when the poll is high (the highest point), flexed, and relaxed. The relaxation at the poll results from the relaxation of the jaw.

Consequently, any dressage should start by working the "mise en main." At a halt first, in hand against the wall; then forward, always

Fig. 22 - The working posture. The horse is collecetd; maximum slanting of pelvis; yet no lowering of the haunches.

in hand, forward movement bringing about a collected, hence diagonal, walk. Then the "mise en main" should be worked from horseback, at a halt and then slow and progressively more and more "enlarged" gaits. Keeping the "mise en main" unaltered is the guarantee of balance, the one and only balance, which Baucher would call the balance "of the first genre."

With a horse who has been rid of his vertebral blockings, the "mise en main" is realized in no time, since the horse will yield immediately and nicely in his mouth (equipped with a simple snaffle) because the possible causes for a resistance have been eliminated.

Placing the head at the optimal height is a matter of tact; the rider should feel when the elevation of the neck creates the maximal engagement of the pelvis.

When this "mise en main" is correctly kept at a halt or slow gaits, it is of course most important to take chances and try to keep it in larger and larger gaits.

Progression

The progression to follow will be determined by the horse. Most often, piaffe will appear first. In the beginning of the training, piaffe should not be cultivated for its own sake, but as a manifestation of activity in a collected attitude. Not only should one teach a horse how to piaffe, one should also teach him, in the first place, how to quit piaffing, since piaffing may become an evasion. But all this is a matter of tact; nobody has ever said that equitation was easy, although it becomes easy...after years and years of arduous study.

Walk and canter strike-offs should be preferred over trot, since trot does not by itself foster collection, whereas "counted walk" (which eventually becomes "school walk") and repeated canter departs will help (for the definition of "counted walk," see Appendix 5, First Level Test One, paragraph 6). It is important to get the "passage" rapidly if possible, because it will help greatly in improving the trot; one just has to "infuse" some passage into the trot to render it spectacular. Trot is a result, not a means.

Likewise for transitions; they are not a means, but a result. When light in hand, a horse passes in no time from an extended canter to a canter in place (I don't use the expression collected canter, since collection was also present in the extended canter).

Canter pirouettes, when a horse is light in hand, are mere formalities. They are performed on quasi looped reins and induced through a simple movement of the rider's body. Horses love it.

Now look at the heavy, laborious pirouettes realized by those horses who have been pushed forward at the beginning of their training, irrespective of their state of collection.

However, the purpose of this book is not to describe in detail the riding proceedings which allow one to better realize such or such a movement. For this, there are numerous good books (may I suggest my **Another Horsemanship**, with only one "erratum": the book reads that in a canter pirouette the rider's weight should be placed to the outside, whereas it should bear slightly inside).

And even if you don't find these books, or have no riding teacher, your horse will tell you what to do next.

One last question: since there is no rigid progression, what about the different "levels" of competitive dressage?

Well, it's my belief that those levels are more for the riders than for the horses. It is obvious that beginner riders cannot ride a Grand Prix. They have to start with First Level Test One. As for the horses, really, they know only two levels. The first level is when they are still not correctly muscled and cannot keep the balance in all their evolutions. This level presents no interest whatsoever. The second level is when a horse is correctly muscled in his back, base of the withers, crest of the neck, and rump and can keep collection, hence balance, unaltered in every aspect of his evolutions. Then, everything becomes possible.

The actual progression of tests, from First Level Test One to Grand Prix, was established according to the beliefs of the now prevalent school, which does not make balance a prerequisite, and, as Baucher would say, "works the movement through the movement." It is difficult indeed to squeeze oneself into a program based on a riding philosophy that one questions.

Sacrificing balance to show at First Level, in order to please the judges who believe that, since they want balance to be established progressively, it should not be shown *and tolerated* at a low level, a very shocking proposition indeed, is a waste of time, and an error that perhaps your horse will not forgive you for.

But the more a given level accepts collection, the more the discrepancy lessens, and the more you will feel at ease.

There is, in the 1945 book by Beudant (perhaps the most extraordinary rider of all time) **Main sans jambes**, a great passage in which, after he described all the wonderful movements of "High School" one of his horses, "Mimoun," was performing (some of them absolutely incredible, like counter changes of hand at a counter canter!), he concludes by saying, "But now, 'Mimoun' can do a regular and large trot, a gait which he seemed definitely unfit for at first."

"Mimoun," when Beudant started his training, was so lacking in impulsion that "a blow on the croup with a big stick, if strong enough, can make him jump forward, but he stops smack as soon as his feet touch ground, without any elasticity." And Beudant would add "that he could absolutely not set this animal into a trot, a gait which he seems totally incapable of."

The other method, the one acknowledged by the FEI nowadays, which works "the movement by the movement," would, of course, have gotten nothing out of "Mimoun". Because if the great Beudant himself could not get a trot from "Mimoun," who would have? You will tell me, "Get rid of the horse and choose a better one!" That's probably valid for whoever wants to practice competitive dressage, but that certainly does not satisfy the true "aficionado."

On the other hand, teaching a horse first how to piaffe and then to passage in order to some day get a regular trot from him seems rather farfetched. And at any rate, it can only be implemented by seasoned riders. How have these riders acquired their experience? By being started with the other method, becoming disappointed by it, evaluating its flaws, and then changing course radically.

This is the problem with Baucherism: it does not lend itself easily to a progression, all the more so as every horse is different.

However, being too radical would not help, and therefore I have devised a simple progression of exercises, broken down into three levels, which could allow the riders with a competitive mind, but fond of lightness, to look for the judgements of their peers, or elders. See Appendixes 4 and 5.

Riding style

The French riding terminology uses two different terms to characterize the relationship between a rider's hand and a horse's mouth: "contact" and "appui." There is "contact" when the rein is taut, ever so slightly. There can be "contact" on the mere weight of the reins.

When this contact becomes more or less strong, implying a muscular resistance from the rider's hand, it becomes "appui," which we can translate as "leaning" (from the horse's point of view) or "support" (from the rider's point of view). "Appui" applies more to resistances of weight (waged downwards) than to resistances of force, carried on more or less horizontally. With "appui," these resistances of weight, instead of being fought, are accepted as a part of the whole equestrian process.

"Contact" in English is ambiguous, since it can mean either light contact or bearing. It does not give any account of the quality and intensity of the tension in the rein. Therefore the reader will allow me to use the French word "appui."

Appui is quite present in the German riding. The baroque masters mention it. La Guérinière, the Johann Sebastian Bach of baroque riding (the men were born three years apart and died one year apart from each other) defines it in this way: "Appui is the feeling produced by the action of the bridle in the rider's hand, and conversely the action operated on the horse's bars by the rider's hand" (**Ecole de Cavalerie**, 1769 edition, p. 131, translation is mine). La Guérinière defines three stages for "appui" (firm, light, and temperate) corresponding to three stages for the hand action (light, soft, and firm).

All this is not very clear and belongs more in the field of poetry than in the field of exact science.

The danger of this notion of "appui" is that it is not quantitative. Some riding instructors nowadays find that twenty pounds in each hand is an acceptable "appui." Some advise more.

Baucher himself, on some occasions, used the expression "appui ferme et lèger" ("firm and light appui"), probably to placate his contemporaries, or make himself understood by them, but it is obvious that all his endeavors aimed at killing this notion of "appui," since he focused more and more on the flexion of the jaw, and since lightness was his motto.

Incidentally, let's notice that the same ambivalence reins in La Guérinière's theory, since the expression "the weight of the reins" was coined by La Guérinière himself.

If we believe that the "mise en main," which implies the yielding of the jaw, is the token of balance, then we have to admit that "appui," which denies the very idea of jaw yielding, *is always the accepted share of imbalance.* Certainly, a half-halt is a means to restore balance, but you will notice that after a half-halt, there should be no more "appui."

I have already dealt in part with this subject in the chapter "Two Different Horsemanships."

The riding style I will describe in the present chapter is concerned with, and indispensable to, riding in lightness.

Four principles preside over riding in lightness: release of the aids, separation of the aids, moderation of the aids, and optimization of orders.

Release of the aids means that the aids should quit as soon as they have acknowledged a response. They bring about, restore, transform; they never maintain.

Separation of the aids means that they should be implemented separately, as much as possible. At any rate, they should not contradict each other. In other words, one may not use restrictive aids and propulsive aids at the same time. This principle extends to the use of the reins, which should not contradict each other.

Moderation of the aids states that the aids should not trespass a certain threshold, of intensity for leg actions, of duration (half a second) for hand actions.

Optimization of orders means that one should not give an order without having carefully set the conditions for its optimal execution.

Everybody will agree on this latter proposition. On the other hand, if we consider it broadly, it encompasses the other three principles, since they deal with schooling the aids, in order to "hone" them to an extreme of efficiency, which can be considered a condition for an optimal execution of the orders. Hence any other horsemanship is wrong, or to say the least, imperfect.

To demonstrate the validity of the first three principles enunciated above, one has to recollect memories about the experiences of Pavlov on conditioned reflexes. Pavlov took a dog and presented it with a piece of meat to make it salivate, in the meantime ringing a bell on a given pitch. The meat was a natural trigger to salivation, itself a natural reflex.

After eighty such experiments, the meat would no longer be necessary to trigger salivation; the bell alone would do the job. The bell had been, so to say, "loaded" with the meaning of the meat. It had become an artificial trigger for the reflex. The reflex itself was no longer natural, but "conditioned."

Let's now consider the rider's legs, to start with. Physiologically, their action is absolutely not impulsive, since a young horse would rather tend to "cringe" when they are used, though this "cringing" effect is negligible, and we can consider the legs a neutral signal which can be loaded with any significance, depending on the effect of any natural trigger one decides to associate with it.

Since we want the leg to become impulsive, we will choose a whip as a natural trigger and associate it with the indication of the leg. Progressively, the leg will be loaded with the meaning of the whip, *a natural trigger*, and become *an artificial trigger*. This is basic training for a young horse.

Let's notice that the strength of the response is not in proportion to the strength of the solicitation. When the conditioning is at its peak, a very light ringing of the bell will suffice to make a dog salivate. Likewise, a simple indication of the legs (the "wind of the boot") will suffice to motivate a horse forward.

A conditioning, unfortunately, is not forever. It undergoes a phase of oblivion, during which ringing the bell stronger and stronger will be to no avail; the conditioning will have to be "refreshed." In Pavlov's experiments, only four sessions were enough to "recondition" a dog, whereas eighty were necessary to condition it in the first place.

Any conditioning can be erased by another, if the nature of the natural trigger changes. For instance, if we condition the leg action to trigger the forward movement, and if we systematically remove our leg from the horse's sides as soon as the movement has been started, the leg will mean acceleration. But if we keep our leg on as the horse proceeds forward, the leg will be demoted from vector acceleration to vector speed. And as increasing the strength of the leg action (as increasing the intensity of the bell's ringing) will not have any effect on the intensity of the answer, we are in a rut, and spurs (a natural, although imperfect, trigger for impulsion) will have to be used constantly. This is what we see happening on the dressage rectangles, where the horses are spurred at each and every step and each and every stride.

But although the spurs have some natural impulsive effect, their continual use does not make much sense as well. Let me come up with a comparison. In all the armies of the world, an order comprises two parts: preparation first, and then execution. For instance: "Forward..." (preparation) "March!" (execution). Now, one does not imagine a battalion commander saying "March!", "March!", "March!", "March!", "March!", "March!", etc..., and his battalion stopping when, out of breath, he cannot go on shouting "March!" anymore. Yet this is exactly what we do when we use our legs to maintain a movement, instead of using them only to start the movement.

Besides, the horse will become blunt to the spurs as well, if they are used too systematically.

This shows the necessity of the release of the legs as soon as their action has been understood and responded to by the horse.

The same applies for hand actions. If they maintain a speed, they will devaluate their power. If they maintain a neck position, the rider's muscles are put to work rather than the horse's. In any case, the hand action has to be released, telling the horse that *he*, and not the rider, has to maintain position and action.

Releasing the aids is a contract proposed to a horse to make him understand that he has to collaborate and fulfill his part of the agreement.

A last comparison to make myself better understood, if necessary. When you have a trinket whose balance is precarious when set on a shelf, you are obliged to quit touching it if you want to ascertain that the said trinket is stable. It is the same for a horse: the aids have to quit in order to establish that the horse is in the proper balance. If he is not, he will "fall" in one direction or another, and the aids will have to restore position and/or action. They will do so time and again, until the horse understands what his job is and takes it in charge; for there is a big difference between a trinket and a horse: the horse has a brain.

Let's now tackle the problem of separation of the aids. First, a combined action of the aids will give the horse a blurry picture of what the rider means; "go - don't go," in the hope that the horse will understand "collect," is a very questionable set of orders. But there is more: since the reins may claim some natural effect, and since the legs have none, systematically using hands and legs together will load the latter with the meaning of the former, and the horse will understand that, after all, the legs don't mean acceleration but deceleration.

Then the rider, believing that the horse is "lazy," will spur him, partially reconditioning the horse to an impulsive meaning of the legs, and the horse will so "progress" in his training, tossed about between two conflicting meanings for the leg.

The artificial character of the rider's legs effect explains why they should not be used forcefully (and we are now dealing with the third principle, that of moderation of the aids). The legs act ex-quality, not ex-quantity. When a horse does not answer the legs, it is not because he does not "hear" the legs; it is because he does not understand their meaning, or at any rate, he still has doubts about it.

If you don't understand Greek, shouting won't help; you must learn Greek first. And then there's no reason to shout. It's the same with the horse; he has to learn the language of the legs, and it is rather easy, since it is comprised of only one word: "Go!" Though even the horse should understand what the word means.

I have said that the hand may claim some natural, physiological restraining effect. But since this effect is due to the pain brought about in the horse's mouth by the action of the bit, it is not likely to be received kindly, more so with the young horse. That's why the hand action should be pulsated in order to quit as soon as the horse is organizing himself against it. Picking up the "rhythm" will allow one to restrain any horse in no time; it is a question of practice and tact.

Let's now examine the fourth principle, that of "optimization of orders." It concerns impulsion. Impulsion relies on two factors: communication and balance. Communication first: a horse has to understand the language of the aids. That was the domain of the first three principles.

Considering balance now. Imbalance is certainly a major obstacle to impulsion, so balance should be established first, and we know that the "mise en main" ("bringing in hand") is the absolute token for absolute balance.

The rider's position contributes to the achievement of the riding performance. The legs should be positioned through their mere weight, so they not be the setting of any contraction. These contractions diminish the rider's ability to use his/her aids optimally and are felt by the horse, who reacts by "cringing."

The rider's hands should not be clenched on the reins; they should be held between thumb and index, the other fingers being set "ajar" on the reins. This position allows one to "give" (by opening the fingers still more), "resist" (by maintaining the fingers' position), or "take" (by clenching the fingers). The hand language becomes subtle, and the reins are no longer mere handles, simply meant to secure the rider firmly in the saddle.

The reins should be allowed to slide between the rider's fingers if necessary; control is restored by the mere clenching of the thumb over the index, when needed.

The hands should not be kept too much apart.

The upper body should be relaxed (but not collapsed), and the rider's back should be slightly arched. Arching the back fosters vertical impulsion. Rounding the back fosters horizontal impulsion. Round your back in the up transitions; arch it in the down transitions.

At a halt, asking for a jaw flexion and then arching the back will most often create collection. This is the best "effet d'ensemble" I know of.

Questioning some aspects
of the FEI (i.e., German) method

Most often, and even at an Olympic level, one can see riders spurring their horses at every stride of trot, passage, or canter. One can see conspicuous aids, in canter flying changes of lead for instance, and also in piaffes, where the riders often seem to piaffe more than the horses. This is because the legs have lost any impulsive effect, through ignorance of the principles of release, separation, and moderation of the aids. The very idea of "maintenance aids," "supporting aids," works against impulsion and balance. It is an error to take the effect of the aids for granted; they draw their convincing power from a conditioning, more so the legs, and this conditioning is fragile, but this misconception is still widely spread.

Furthermore, the requirement for a horse to be "connected," that is, to establish or accept a strong contact with the rider's hands, is very detrimental to balance; it is also detrimental to the horse's vertebral structure, which I have demonstrated in this book.

"Connection" of the horse's mouth to the rider's hand by anything else than the weight of the reins amounts to lack of self-carriage.

Lack of self-carriage, in turn, renders the canter pirouettes laborious.

The use of the inside leg to create lateral bending (which, I have demonstrated, tends to hollow the horse's back, see chapter "Probable Causes for Vertebral Blockings"), as well as the denial of the use of the indirect rein, results in the horses' never coming correctly into the corners, and haunches skidding out in the voltes.

But there is an aspect of German horsemanship on which I would like to focus more particularly, that of "rhythm."

The Germans insist strongly on the notion of "rhythm" in equitation, but here as in all the other aspects of their method, they tackle the problem from the outside instead of tackling it from the inside. If balance is perfect, the gait will be perfect in all its aspects, especially the rhythm. But imposing the rhythm through a constant bombardment from the aids, besides the fact that it will numb and stupefy the horse, will not create balance.

And this all the less so as the rhythm imposed by the rider will not, as a rule, be the natural rhythm of the horse. The horse will constantly be driven "out of his pace," as they say in sporting horsemanship. This eagerness of the rider of the German School to ceaselessly hustle his/her horse under the pretense of "energy" is one of the fundamental flaws of this school. At a collected walk, for instance, the judges will require a horse to shorten his stride while he accelerates his cadence. This is highly unnatural, and it is why so many horses end up ambling (pacing), which they will be reproached for, to boot! Collection should never shrink a gait; it should only slow its rhythm.

The truth lies in the Baucherist motto, "Give the position first, and then let the horse do" ("Placer et laisser faire"). One should let the horse express himself in all his majesty and in the cadence which is his.

APPENDIXES

Appendix 1

More on the Flexion of the Jaw

The flexion of the jaw was introduced at the beginning of this book. It has been present all along its course, since it is at the very core of "lightness." Given its importance, more technical details are certainly not superfluous.

Yet details, however important, have to be inserted in a whole. Some "cement" is necessary; this "cement" is the gist of the matter, which has already been exposed in the main part of the book. Therefore, some repetitions are inevitable.

The lines hereunder are excerpts from an article I wrote on that subject for Issue #8 of the magazine *Riding in Lightness*.

The flexion of the jaw is a very little understood procedure. Very few people know what it is, how to get it, what results it produces, and why. And when they understand all of the above, guess what? They still don't use it! So let's examine these points in the order they came.

1) What is the flexion of the jaw?

The flexion of the jaw is, as it happens, a flexion of the TMJ (the temporo-mandibular joint), meant to temporarily annul the contractions that may happen in this area. This joint is located circa two inches behind the eye, under the base of the ear, and whilst we are focusing strongly on the bit and the lower part of the mouth, the real thing happens high in the head, a good twelve inches away from the bit.

The term "flexion" is a little misleading, since the opening of the jaw "per se" is not what is being looked for (although it is part of the process). Our purpose is to relax that joint, to prevent it from being contracted, to "discontract" it (the word does not exist in English, but it would be the exact translation of the French "décontracter").

In the flexion of the jaw, the horse "lets go" of the bit. This should not frighten you. It is about a *momentary* loss of contact whereby the horse "savors" the bits, making them "jingle." The tongue goes up and down several times, which shows, incidentally, that the flexion of the jaw is the sure fire remedy for "curled tongues."

Many words have been used to describe the flexion of the jaw: mobility of the jaw, yielding of the jaw, mobility of the tongue… Let me quote the two most famous. General L'Hotte speaks of a "light murmur." And Captain Etienne Beudant has this admirable expression: the horse "smiles." Indeed, it is absolutely impossible to smile and contract the jaws at the same time. As we clench our teeth, we can grin, but we cannot smile.

2) How to get it?

Contractions can't be seen, but they can be felt. To help my students understand what sensation they have to look for, I ask them to take my hand and press it strongly; on my side, I resist their pressure by stiffening my hand. Then I tell them that I will give up resisting and that they will certainly feel the difference. It is very reassuring to notice that every time I give up on my resisting, the student instinctively quits squeezing, which is exactly what should happen when a horse yields in his mouth. This shows that feeling the jaw flexion is within everybody's reach.

The snag lies in being in a position to yield when a pressure is applied, not on somebody's hand, but on the reins. When you press (squeeze) my hand, *you certainly don't pull.* But a rein is much smaller, thinner, than my hand. *You have to learn how to squeeze the rein and not pull on it.*

You will perhaps tell me, "And what is the big deal if I pull? I am smart enough to yield when the horse yields."

Well, you think that you are smart enough, and I don't doubt for one minute your good intentions. But you are not. Nobody is.

To show my students the limitations of our reflexes, I generally come up with an old trick that I have described time and again in articles and books, lectures and clinics, and that I will one more time describe here. It consists of holding a one dollar bill vertically (upright) as another person places two fingers of a hand, thumb and index, on either side, one inch apart and at mid-height of the bill.

Then I drop the bill, and it so happens that the person can *never* grab it. Because it takes a fraction of a second for the person to realize that I have dropped the bill, one other fraction of a second to send the order to "grab" to the muscles of the fingers, and one more fraction of a second for the fingers to execute the order. Those three fractions of a second added together amount to too much time; the bill is already out of reach.

This illustrates the human's relative slowness. As compared to the horse's reflexes, we are no match. For instance, I am on horseback, with long reins, happy and lost in my thoughts, and something happens all of a sudden, an explosion for instance. The horse will have noticed it, reacted to it, and come back to calm when I myself am only at the stage of realizing that an explosion has occurred. I am slow; he was not.

When we apply a traction on the reins, the horse reacts most often by pulling in the other direction. Then if we maintain that pressure, he will try several other answers, move his lower jaw sideways from right to left and left to right, try to snatch out the reins, lift his head, etc... One of these reactions may be, we hope, that he will momentarily yield by "letting go" of the bit. He should then be rewarded instantaneously, so that he understands that this was the good answer, and for that we cannot rely on our reflexes, whatever our good will. The release has to be *automatic* and not depend on us. This will happen if we apply a *pressure* on the reins and not a *traction*. A traction implies the action of the arm; a pressure implies only the action of the fingers. If you pull with your arm, you won't control your action as the horse yields, because one more time, our reflexes are too slow; there will be a "recoil" effect, and the horse will be punished. He will then think that yielding was not the good answer. If you press with your fingers, your yielding will certainly be as slow, but there will be no "recoil," since you were applying *to the rein* (with your fist) and not to the mouth (with your arm). Applying to the rein only was, of course, an indirect way of applying to the horse's mouth, but in a very subtle—although sometimes very powerful—way.

This way of doing is called "the fixed hand." A "fixed" hand is a hand that refuses to be carried away in any direction: forward, by the traction of the horse; backward, by the possible "recoil" resulting from the yielding of the mouth. The "fixed" hand is not fixed with respect to the horse's body, like side reins, or with respect to the horse's mouth, as when we go over a jump. It is fixed *with respect to itself,* meaning that it is not moved by the resistance, or by the yielding, of the jaw.

The actions of reins can be divided into two categories: the "drawer" actions (pulling with your arm to open a drawer) and the "lemon" action (squeezing with the fist in order to extract juice). When you pull on a drawer, if it resists, you will very likely be set off balance if it yields all of a sudden; perhaps you will fall. If you squeeze a lemon, whatever the resistance of the lemon, you won't fall when it yields. No one has ever seen anybody fall by squeezing a lemon.

As a rule, the hand actions should follow the pattern "drawer-lemon." "Drawer" first, that is, a traction from the arms, in order to "feel" the horse's mouth. Then, "lemon," that is, a squeezing with the fingers on the reins, to provoke the yielding of the mouth. When you do "drawer," you don't do "lemon," and when you do "lemon," you don't do "drawer." The error of many riders is to do "drawer" first to get the contact with the mouth, and then to add one strong "drawer" to get the mouth to yield. They thus pull with the arm, the horse won't be rewarded on time upon yielding, and there will be a fight. You perhaps will "win" that fight, but that will be at the price of an irritated horse and a clattering mouth, and the good souls of the "other school" will tell you, "You see, I told you!"

To make myself, I hope, definitively understood, I will use one last comparison: imagine you have to pull out a stump in your backyard, and that you have a tractor equipped with a winch, plus a chain, at your disposal. You will first fix the chain, one way or another, to the stump. But the chain is heavy; it is not "taut." To tighten it, you will move the tractor forward. This represents the first "drawer" action, the action of the arm. Then you can do two things: the wrong one or the right one.

The wrong one consists of going on pulling with the tractor: when the stump yields, if it does, the tractor will be projected forward before you get the reflex to stop it. This compares to the first action I just described, the "drawer-drawer" action.

The right way consists of stopping the tractor as soon as the chain is taut (quit using the arm), and then use the winch (the squeezing with the fist). When the stump yields, if it does, the tractor will not be projected forward, since its wheels were not involved in the process.

Most riders know that they have a tractor (their arms) but do not realize that they also have a winch (their fingers).

Today's riders are taught that their fingers should be once and for all and beforehand (no pun intended, although the fingers are always before...hand), clenched onto the reins. Therefore, they have lost their "winch" possibilities. They have only the tractor! So they pull, and the horse responds by pulling! What's left for them? Half-halt and push with the legs. And good day to you and come and see me again when you have recovered your breath.

On the contrary, the reins must be held *between thumb and index finger*, the other fingers being *ajar*, the "pinky" pointing more or less toward the horse's mouth. Only this position of hand can allow one to perform the three stages described by La Guérinière (**Ecole de Cavalerie**, 1731) of the "light hand" (fingers open), the "soft hand" (fingers ajar), and the "firm hand" (fingers clenched). Modern riders know only the "firm hand." It is a lack of opportunity which renders their equitation coarse.

People believe that they will lose the contact when they open the fingers, but it is not so if they follow my advice, i.e., to constantly keep the reins held, strongly if needed, between thumb and index. And there is the beauty of the thing, that one can open the fingers, realizing the "light hand," while in the meantime squeezing the "pincer" thumb-index in order to keep control.

Even when they are free from vertebral blockings, many horses won't freely flex their jaw at first, more so when a pattern of contractions has settled in for a long time. Certainly the rider needs an education in the flexion of the jaw, but so does the horse.

For this, you can, of course, take Baucher's book and practice all the flexions described in it. They are certainly very useful. But I will give you here two or three very simple ways.

First: on foot, face the horse, take both snaffle rings with both thumbs, and push up, toward the joint between second and third vertebrae (that is to say, by and large, following the natural direction of the mouth itself, a little lower). Push steadily, progressively, strongly if necessary, but please introduce this strength gram by gram! When the horse yields, relax, and drop your thumbs.

Second: if this does not work, facing the horse, push the snaffle (or the curb bit) vertically (upright) against the upper palate of the horse; that is, apply the pressure not to the lower jaw but to the upper jaw. The same recommendations apply as for the first procedure described here above. Don't hesitate to go as high as needed. You will feel the horse yield when he quits pushing down on the bit. Release immediately, and drop the bit. The horse's head then falls in a vertical or thereabouts direction.

After each of these flexions, take advantage of the horse's positive answer and try to foster the same result by applying a traction on the reins, perpendicular to the mouth.

Third: in hand, or from horseback. Bend the horse's head laterally, to an extreme, while fostering a "rotation" of the line of the ears, that is to say, the outside ear should be lower than the inside ear. Wait until the horse flexes his mouth. Resist, don't pull. Drop your action immediately upon the horse's yielding.

This seemingly "unorthodox" flexion is physiologically correct, as results from the "tri-dimensional law" presented in this book (see chapter "Manipulations: Three Laws, Plus One"). It helps the horse's back to rise.

When the horse has been initiated to the jaw flexion through these exercises, this flexion is asked for, from horseback, by applying a *steady*, progressive hand action, which Baucher and his students of the second "manner" would call a "slow force." This action may possibly be strong in the end, depending on the horse's resistance, but you should establish it gram by gram, by squeezing your fingers on the rein, "in a convulsive manner if necessary" (Beudant), the hand remaining totally fixed.

This action cannot be confused by the horse with the hand (and seat) action destined to slow, since this latter should be *pulsated* (lasting less than one half second, and reiterated), whereas the "slow force" is steady and progressive.

For that matter, you have to establish a convention with your horse. This convention will be all the more rapidly established as, when you are asking for a flexion in motion, if the horse resists, you will stop him (pulsated actions), relax the jaw at a halt (steady resistance), and then start the movement again.

3) What results can we expect from a jaw flexion?

They are immeasurable.

The flexion of the jaw resonates in the whole body of the horse. Put a close contact saddle on your horse and, at a halt, ask for a jaw flexion: you will feel the muscles of the horse's back *move* under your seat, an indication that something big is happening.

The flexion of the jaw destroys all the resistances. Take for instance a horse who, at a halt is reluctant to move his haunches to the right or the left under the pressure of a single leg. Then ask for a jaw flexion, and upon its coming, use your single leg: the haunches will yield nicely. Take a horse who is reluctant to back up. Then ask for a deep, thorough yielding of the mouth, with the bit jingling, etc., and upon its coming, softly raise one hand: the horse will back up, and to boot, the diagonal to move first will be that on the same side as the hand action.

The flexion of the jaw is a token of balance. Often, on the occasion of my clinics, I have to ride horses whose balance is faulty, and I am sometimes obliged to elevate their necks quite a lot to get that balance. But as soon as the horse understands that he must yield with his mouth, the elevation of the head no longer matters; the horse remains in the proper balance. One can thus ride with looped reins on a quiet, cadenced, and self-impulsed horse. Riding with looped reins on a contracted horse, i.e., abandoning the horse on the forehand without any preparation, may be life threatening. Riding with looped reins on a horse who remains seated on the haunches thanks to the yielding of the jaw is heaven.

The flexion of the jaw is the tool for the "mise en main" ("bringing in hand"), which establishes and keeps collection.

4) Why does it work?

A hardship that almost every young boy playing soccer at school will experience at least once in his lifetime is being hit by the ball in his groin area. Believe me, it hurts. Then he will be told to go and urinate immediately (it is supposed to help). Yes, but what if he can't, because it hurts so much? Then they will tell him to swallow his saliva, and lo and behold, that makes the thing more possible. In other words, the fact of swallowing the saliva relaxes all the other sphincters. It has an altogether relaxing action.

Given the fact that a horse is centered quite a lot on his stomach (What is a horse? A digestive tube with something around it), this fact may be still more prevalent as concerns the equine. I don't doubt that the up and down movement of the tongue, accompanied by a swallowing of the saliva, resonates upon the whole autonomic nervous system of the horse. But how? That would have to be studied seriously by a veterinarian.

But let me come up here with a more immediate explanation.

The flexion of the jaw, we have seen, applies to the TMJ. The relevant area lies right under the horse's ears. In this area, there are three joints very close to each other: the temporo-mandibular joint, the "atlanto-occipital" joint (between the occiput, on the back of the skull, and the "atlas," the first cervical vertebra), and the "atlas-axis" joint, the joint between the first two cervical vertebrae ("axis" is the name given to the second cervical vertebra). Those joints are very important. For instance, it is at the level of the "atlas-axis" joint, between the first two cervical vertebrae, that the head of the horse turns to the right or the left; it is this joint that allows this movement, and not the joint between atlas and skull.

This latter joint, on the other hand, allows the flexion of the head in a vertical (or "sagittal") plane, the famed "ramener." In other words, when a horse says "yes" (nods), he does it with the "atlanto-occipital" joint, but when he says "no," the movement happens at the level of the "atlas-axis" joint, one vertebra farther back. When a horse says "no," he does it with his head and atlas moving together; in other words, it is the atlas that says "no" and not the head directly; the head is just carried away by the movement of the atlas. (Incidentally, there is some irony in the fact that so many riders hope that the horse is going to say "yes" and get his "ramener" in making him say "no" by pulling alternately on the reins...but after all, everybody knows that two negations amount to an affirmation!)

Those three joints form a "triangle" of small dimension: the distance between the TMJ and the "atlanto-occipital" joint is perhaps 2 inches, and the distance between the "atlanto-occipital" joint and the "atlas-axis" joint equals the length of the first vertebra, to wit, perhaps three to four inches (Fig. 23). Because of this proximity, it is impossible to think that if the TMJ is "locked," the play of the other

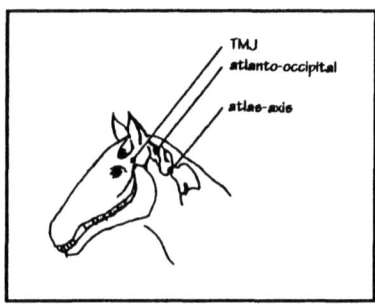

Fig. 23 - Three joints in the poll area.

two joints is going to be supple and easy. Now, this play is most important for the good functioning of the equine machinery, if only because when the poll is high, flexed, and relaxed (through the relaxation of the TMJ), a position which is called "mise en main" ("bringing in hand") *the horse is ipso facto collected*, which means that he "tips" his butt under and raises his rib cage between the shoulders (without the intervention of his rider's legs).

This latter observation is the basis for the Baucherist doctrine, which looks for the "mise en main" ("bringing in hand") at a halt first, then at slow gaits, and progressively endeavors to keep it unaltered in the more extended gaits as well. The persistence of the "mise en main" is the guarantee of the persistence of balance, a perfect balance, resulting from the general posture of the horse who maintains his rib cage elevated between the shoulders and his pelvic area "tipped under." This is the balance that Baucher would call "equilibrium of the first genre" in the 1864 edition of his Method, which marks the official start of the "Second Manner."

This sets in evidence the importance of the jaw flexion, for without it there is no "mise en main" ("bringing in hand") and with no "mise en main," there is no real collection, that is, a collection based on lightness.

5) How come the jaw flexion is so overlooked?

The notion of "flexion of the jaw" was introduced by Baucher in the middle of the XIXth century.

The technique itself underwent some vicissitudes in the course of Baucher's quest. Baucher started with using a whole set of lateral flexions *of the neck*, which were considered as completed only when the horse would relax his jaw (making the bits "jingle").

The lateral flexions were meant to prepare the "direct" (fore and aft) flexion. It was a flexion *of the poll* which itself had to be accompanied by a yielding of the jaw. Later on, in the direct flexion of the "second manner," the jaw had to yield *before* the poll. This direct flexion was prepared for by "semi-lateral" flexions of the neck, the head being positioned high.

Whereas Baucherism took hold in France, the Germans never subscribed to it; they even vilified it. At the time of the creation of the FEI, their representatives were, of course, fully aware that this jaw flexion technique was quite prevalent in the French way, and since the French Riding School was at that time still very prestigious, they had no other choice than to pay lip service to it (lip service is a very fitting word when it comes to flexion of the...jaw).

The political and cultural battle turned, as everybody knows, to the advantage of the Germans, whose influence is now overwhelming in dressage. Therefore, in the last twenty years, as dressage developed rapidly, the only gospel that was preached was the German gospel, which ignores, or even condemns, the notion of jaw flexion.

In the USA, only the riders of the old American School, that of Fort Riley, knew and practiced the flexion of the jaw. Their influence, like that of the French School, is now reduced to a homeopathic level.

There is also a psychological aspect in the matter. The Germans like to control, and for this they want their horses firmly hooked on the bit (although I believe that light in hand, a horse is more disciplined than when bearing on the bit). This in turn will require sometimes conspicuous aids, which will not discourage a German rider.

As for the independent thinkers and researchers, their opinion on the flexion of the jaw will depend on the results they got when they first experienced it. Now, not all horses react in the same way to it; serious vertebral blockings render it sometimes difficult and at any rate less productive.

As we have seen, the direct flexion of the jaw is the base for the "mise en main," realized when the poll is high, flexed, and relaxed (through the relaxation of the TMJ). This entails a lifting of the withers and a "tipping under" of the pelvis. This posture defines collection.

Some (many) will tell you that the elevation of the withers does not exist, that it is only relative to the lowering of the haunches; in other words, that it is an optical illusion. They are wrong, since there exists a muscle, the "serratus costalis," whose job it is to elevate the rib cage between the shoulders. This muscle originates in the upper inner part of the shoulder blade and is inserted down on the 8 to 9 first ribs of the horse. When this muscle contracts itself, the rib cage is pushed up. There is no denying this.

Still, one can understand those who don't acknowledge this fact. It so happens that they have dealt mostly with horses whose vertebral column, more so in its cervical segment, is the setting of vertebral blockings. As a result, their withers lose their ability to rise. Most often, these blockings result from forceful riding: immoderate use of side-reins, head set too low, strong contact with the rider's hands.

Such horses are often reluctant to give a "direct" jaw flexion, because they are in pain, or at least they feel uneasy. Conversely, the direct flexion of the jaw will not take care of these blockings. One will then have to resort to Baucher's lateral flexions, whereby the jaw is asked to yield, upon the horse's neck being laterally bent, the line of the ears remaining horizontal. Time and again, I have observed that the flexions of Baucher in his first, as well as in his second, "manner," if well performed and regularly repeated, will release the possible vertebral blockings of the cervical vertebrae, and even of the first three thoracic vertebrae. This is quite a lot and is likely to help considerably.

As for blockings situated farther back, behind T3, the flexions of Baucher, as we understand them, do not seem to be efficient, and horses afflicted with them will not raise their withers, or will raise them imperfectly.

It is probably for these horses that Baucher was obliged to artificially bring the hind legs under, with the whip working in hand and the spurs when mounted. The hind legs would come under but with no engagement of the hindquarters, that is, no "tipping under" of the pelvis, this tipping being made impossible by the blockings in the back. In the meantime, in order to alleviate the pain suffered by the horse in this position, the front legs would come under the mass as well. This faulty collection, for which Baucher was reproached in his first "manner", is often to be seen nowadays on the dressage grounds.

Another reason for the abeyance into which the flexion of the jaw has fallen is that it may be tricky to use. People have to learn how not to pull; this requires discipline. Because if we pull, then the flexion of the jaw will turn into "the razor in the monkey's hands." But is it because a scalpel may be dangerous that we should dismiss surgery altogether?

A third reason for this "eclipse" of the flexion of the jaw is more elusive. When I was in France, I had an "aristocratic," or "esoteric," way of teaching the jaw flexion: I would teach it only when I thought the student "worthy" of receiving the message. That was a kind of "initiation" to high horsemanship, a horsemanship, anyway, that would be forever reserved for an elected few.

Coming to the States, where I see some students only twice a year (because of the distances), which imparts to me the obligation of giving as much information as I can in a clinic, I had to change my way, and I started to preach the gospel of the jaw flexion to the lay public, sometimes with a vague feeling of guilt.

But my concern was very unfounded, since I discovered that the flexion of the jaw *is* esoteric *by nature*. You preach it, people listen to you, they believe you, and...they don't do it.

The few who receive the message are the blessed ones... J.C.R.

[113]

Appendix 2

More on the "ramener"

One of the exercises of Baucherism's "second manner" is called "ramener outré," i.e., "uttermost ramener." It consists in tucking in the horse's head to an extreme, the chin touching the chest, and then asking for a jaw flexion. Another exercise of this school consisted in asking for the jaw flexion after having lifted the horse's head to a maximum. These two exercises were total opposites. But then they were combined.

General Faverot de Kerbrech wrote, "The elevation of the neck combined with the ramener outré gives and fixes the true position for the head which, thenceforth, will never be lost, either in large gaits or difficult movements." (**Dressage Méthodique du Cheval de Selle**, p. 187, translation is mine.)

The "ramener outré" was obtained through an opposition of the hand and spurs. This technique is not within everybody's reach.

A simpler technique, anyway, consists of asking for an exaggerated lateral flexion of the neck, the line of the ears "rotating" outward (which, in turn, tends to lift the horse's back) until the horse gives a jaw flexion, then progressively evening up the length of the reins, which leads the horse to straighten up his neck, and then proceeding in the same way on the other side. During the whole process, the jaw should never stiffen. The exercise can be considered successful when the horse passes in a supple manner from a flexion to the left to a flexion to the right and vice versa without lifting his head during the whole process, all the while as he remains light in his mouth.

Thus is the horse overbent, but light.

To subsequently obtain a normal "ramener," the head being vertical and the mouth light (which, in fact, is almost the definition of the "mise en main"), one just has to move the horse forward, and most often, because of the movement, the head is likely to settle in an average position.

But a few horses may present some residual resistance. One then proceeds to the second flexion, i.e., asking for a jaw flexion on a paroxysmal elevation of the neck. When this flexion has been successfully realized, open the fingers, let the reins slide to a reasonable length, and push forward, fingering with the reins if necessary in order to confirm lightness.

Combining these two flexions will produce a classic ramener in no time.

One can practice these two flexions working in hand, in order to obtain or confirm the "mise en main," before asking for a "mobilization in place."

But it would be wrong to try to get anything from these flexions with a horse incapable of lifting his withers. That would be hurting the horse to no avail.

Engagement of the hindquarters and lowering of the haunches

The engagement of the hindquarters is the result of the slanting of the pelvis (forwarding of the point of the buttock). The lowering of the haunches is the result of the flexion of the system "stifle-hock," accompanied or not with the flexion of the coxo-femoral joint ("hip joint").

The two notions are separate, as I have shown in the chapter "Conventional Equestrian Wisdom in the Light of Osteopathy." They may be compounded, as in the perfect collection, but as we will see, they may also be antagonistic.

To cast some light on the subject, it is first necessary to describe the joints of the horse's rear end. There are five of them, if we consider negligible the play in the sacroiliac joint (between sacrum and ilium) and in the joints of the pastern and foot (between first, second, and third phalanges). From top to bottom, we have the sacro-lumbar joint, then the "coxo-femoral joint" ("hip joint"), the stifle, the hock, and the ankle (Fig. 24).

These joints are independent from each other, with the excep-

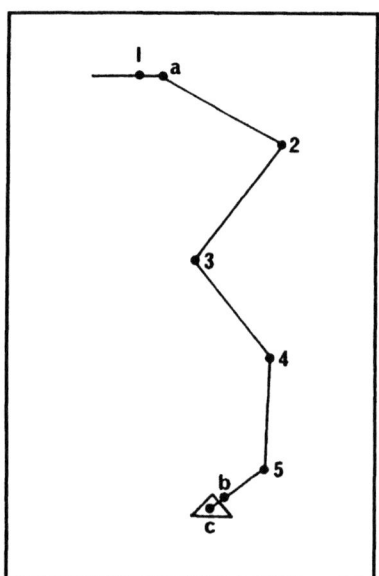

Fig. 24 - Five major joints in the rear end: 1 = sacro-lumbar joint, 2 = Coxo-femural joint, 3 = stifle, 4 = hock, 5 = ankle. For the record: a = sacro-iliac joint, b = pastern joint, c = hoof joint.

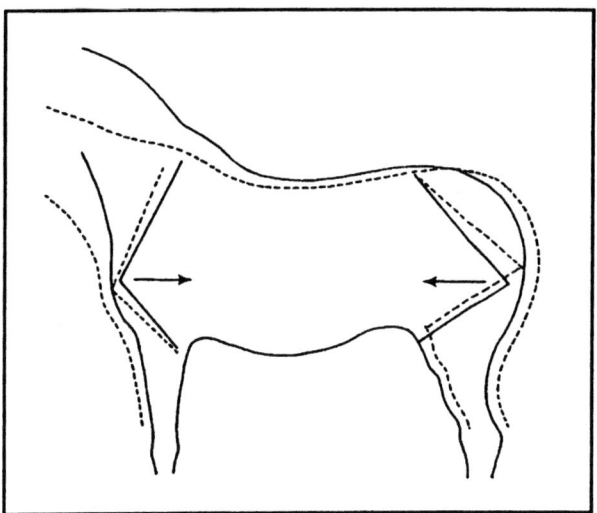

Fig. 25 - Contraction of the medium line.

tion of the stifle and hock, which cannot bend or open independently (when the stifle bends, so does the hock, and vice versa).

A flexion of the sacro-lumbar joint creates a "tipping under" of the pelvis. This results in the engagement of the hindquarters, through the forwarding of the point of the buttock and the subsequent shrinking of the medial line of the horse's body (point of buttock to point of shoulder), i.e., a shrinking of the horse's frame (Fig. 25).

The "coxo-femoral joint" has two constituents: the pelvis and femur. Its flexion (shutting) results from the inclination toward a more horizontal position of each or both of these constituents. So there are three cases possible: either the pelvis alone tends toward a more horizontal position, or the femur alone, or both the femur and pelvis tend toward a more horizontal position. It is to be observed that in the first case as in the third, as the pelvis tends to a more horizontal position, the edge of the buttock backs up, the back flattens, and collection is lost.

As far as flexion is concerned, stifle and hock can be considered as only one joint, by virtue of a system of antagonistic muscles acting like a "pantograph" (or "articulated parallelogram") and situated on both sides of the tibia.

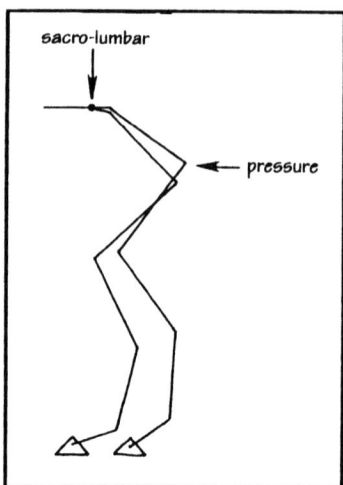

sacro-lumbar

←— pressure

Fig. 26 - Engagement of hindquarters through mere flexion
of the sacro-lumbar joint. No
lowering of the haunches.

There is not much to say about the ankle joint, whose rearward flexibility is much more marked than its forward flexibility; however, this latter plays a great role on the suppleness and "spring" of the gaits, and may add to the possibilities of "lowering" of the haunches.

Let's now consider this whole set of joints in their possible interactions, and let's imagine first that a thrust is applied against the point of buttock ("ischium") with such strength that the horse cannot but yield to it (Fig. 26). The pelvis will rotate, increasing its natural slant. There will be *no* lowering of the croup, as this action is not likely to help in shutting the angle of the coxo-femoral joint, nor does this action have any influence on the possible flexion of the joint system "stifle-hock."

Still, the horse will collect himself, since the forward movement of the point of buttock represents a shortening of the frame and a lifting of the horse's back altogether.

Let's imagine now that the thrust, instead of being applied on the point of buttock, is applied on top of the first sacral vertebra ["jumper's bump"] (Fig. 27). This will induce a rotation of the pelvis, opposite to the one observed in the previous case; the point of the buttock will back up, and the horse's back will flatten. The horse's frame will be lengthened instead of being shortened. This works against collection.

Still, under the pressuere, the three main joints of the rear end, i.e., the coxo-femoral joint, the stifle, and the hock, are likely to flex, entailing a lowering of the haunches. *This shows that the lowering*

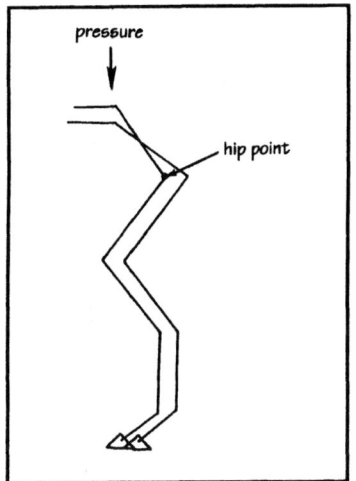

pressure

hip point

Fig. 27 - Lowering of haunches through flexion of the hip joint, point of buttock backs up, croup flattens. Loss of collection.

of the haunches by itself cannot define collection, since in this case the horse is not collected.

What defines collection is the engagement of the hindquarters, i.e., the "tipping under" of the pelvis.

But one can imagine a conjunction of the engagement of the hindquarters with a flexion of the three joints of the rear end. This would define perfect collection. When the horse is performing a levade, the flexions of the sacro-lumbar, stifle, and hock joints are maximal. Only the coxo-femoral doesn't flex (Fig. 28).

Therefore, three cases can be defined:

1) Thorough collection combining the engagement of the hindquarters with the lowering of the haunches; this type of collection

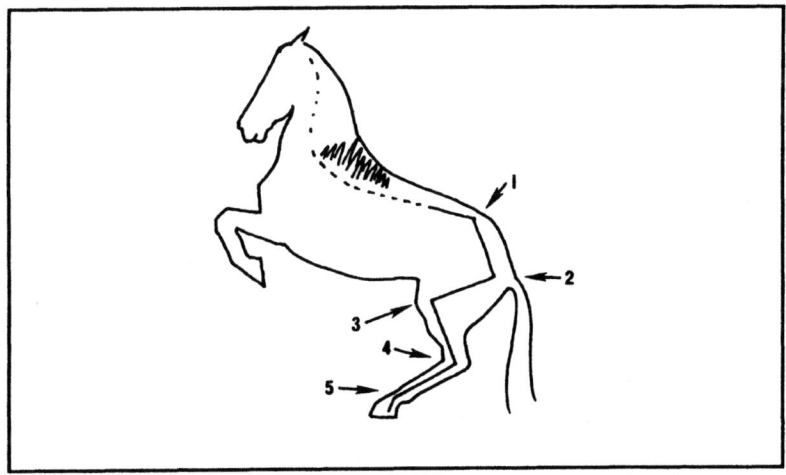

Fig. 28 - Levade. 5 - flexion of ankle, 4-3 - flexion of hock/stifle, 2 - no flexion in the hip joint, 1 - flexion of the sacro-lumbar joint.

[119]

Fig. 29 - Thorough collection.
Poll is at the highest point, withers are lifted, pelvis tilted, stifle and hocks are flexed.

Fig. 30 - Potential drawbacks of the Baroque School.
Rear end crushed through flexion of the three joints (hip, stifle, hock), but no slanting in the pelvis. The back is hollow.

can be observed in the best of both schools, the Baroque school on the one hand and the Baucherist school in its "second manner" (Fig. 29).

2) Working collection resulting from the mere "tilting" of the pelvis, engaging the haunches without flexing them (refer to Fig. 11 and Fig. 22), but in the meantime keeping the withers high.

3) Faulty collection, resulting from a flexion of the haunches without engagement of the hindquarters. This faulty collection, provoking a "crushing" of the rear end and a flattening of the back, was one of the snags of the Baroque school and can still be observed sometimes with the horses of the Spanish School of Vienna (see Fig. 30).

Appendix 4

Propositions of movements and exercises in the spirit of lightness

Although presented in a logical order, and of growing difficulty, the movements and exercises hereunder described are not linked with each other through a design, a text, or a pattern. I don't think it's necessary. A horse (and a rider) who knows his movements must be capable of putting them together in any given order. Transition, in the Baucherist spirit, is a result, that of equilibrium, one and only one equilibrium, the equilibrium "of the first genre." It is not a means; it is an end. It is not by pulling on the reins of an unbalanced horse to momentarily slow down his action, or by stimulating him with the legs to momentarily enlarge it, that one will improve his balance. On the contrary, it is by improving his balance that one will later shorten or widen his action more easily.

The movements and exercises of these three "levels" were put together in tests of twelve movements in order to allow "à la carte" tests. The rider chooses eight movements or exercises and presents them in the order he/she pleases. To pass from one test to the next one, all twelve movements or exercises must have been successfully presented.

The segments between the diverse movements and exercises must be performed in a free walk.

Although piaffe and passage appear only at the third level, a bonus is given to any rider who, at the first level, will show his horse in a piaffe, and passage at the second level. This is because a confirmed rider, working a "sound" horse (i.e., devoid of vertebral blocking), will start the training of his/her horse with "collection in place," the "mold" from which everything should proceed.

As for the "shoulder-in" which appears at the First Level, it is the exercise described by La Guérinière in chapter XI of his book Ecole de Cavalerie, corroborated by the diagram, i.e., a "leg-yielding" associated with a moderate lateral bending.

Last but not least: As often as possible, the show "rectangle" should be equipped with a gate that the rider would have to open from the horse's back in order to enter the competition area. The purpose of dressage is to render a horse mobile and easy to meneuver. And, isn't it a shame to have to acknowledge that nowadays, even Olympic competitors would perhaps be incapable of performiong an exercise that is within the reach of any "4H" youngster?

This explains why each test starts with the words "open the gate."

First (or Introductory) Level (*)

Test 1

Enter (or open the gate, see text above).

Salute, reins completely dropped on the neck.

1.Halt, complete release of the reins (reins on the neck), walk, gather and adjust reins only while walking.

2. Walk, complete release of the reins (reins on the neck), trot, gather and adjust reins only while trotting.

3. Trot, complete release of the reins (reins on the neck), canter, gather and adjust reins only while cantering.

4. Extended free walk, canter depart.

5. Medium walk, canter depart.

6. Halt - counted walk - halt.

7. Halt - counted walk - trot in lightness - walk.

8. Halt - counted walk - canter.

9. Transition trot - walk - trot - walk, etc., without changing speed.

10. Circle on one rein at a walk.

11. Circle on one rein at a trot (drop the other rein).

12. Pass into corners at a walk.

Test 2

Enter (or open the gate, see text above).

Salute, reins completely dropped on the neck.

1. Halt - rein back - halt - rein back - halt - forward at a walk.

2. Shoulder-in along the long side at a walk.

3. Shoulder-in on the diagonal at a trot.

4, Counter shoulder-in on a circle at a walk.

5. Counter shoulder-in on a circle at a trot.

6. Turning around haunches in the bend of shoulder-in at a walk.

7. Turning around shoulders in the bend of half pass (reversed pirouette) at a walk.

8. Counted walk - seat (leg) yielding at a walk.

9. Counted walk - half pass in a counted walk.

10. Shoulder-in at a trot along the long side.

11. Counter change of hand in a shoulder-in at a trot.

12. Pass into corners at a trot.

Test 3

Enter (or open the gate, see text above).

Salute, reins completely dropped on the neck.

1. Walk: circle - shoulder-in away from the circle - circle.

2. Walk: circle - shoulder-in away from the circle - circle - haunches-in on a tangent to the circle.

3. Full side-pass (75 degrees) at a walk along the short side.

4. Waltz (1/2 turn around haunches, 1/2 reversed pirouette, etc.).

5. Pirouette at a walk.

6. Halt - depart into trot.

7. Halt - canter depart.

8. Rein back - depart into trot.

9. Rein back - canter depart.

10. Turning around haunches at a walk - canter depart on the inside lead.

11. Reversed pirouette at a walk - canter depart on the inside lead.

12. Circle on one rein at a canter (drop the other rein).

(*) A bonus will be given to the rider who presents his horse at a piaffe on the occasion of any one of these tests. The movement is not included in the test.

Second(or Intermediate) Level (*)

Test 1

Enter (or open the gate, see text above).

Salute, reins completely dropped on the neck.

1. Halt - rein back - halt - rein back, forward in a trot.

2. Halt - rein back - halt - rein back, forward in a canter.

3. Bend a horse at a halt - forward into a walk on a circle.

4. Bend a horse at a halt - forward into a trot on a circle.

5. Bend a horse at a halt - forward into a canter on a circle.

6. Half pass on a circle (haunches inside) at a walk.

7. Half pass at a trot.

8. Shoulder-in at a canter.

9. Shoulder-in at a trot along the short side, extended trot on the diagonal.

10. Extended canter on the diagonal.

11. Full side-pass (75 degrees) at a walk along the short side, canter depart straight forward on the inside lead.

12. Pass into corners at a canter.

Test 2

Enter (or open the gate, see text above).

Salute, reins completely dropped on the neck.

1. Halt - reins dropped on the neck - canter - gather and adjust the reins only while cantering.

2. Canter - complete release of reins (dropped on neck) on eight strides, on the straight.

3. Canter half pass.

4. Full side-pass (75 degrees) at a canter on a line parallel to the short side of the arena.

5. Half pass at a canter on a circle (haunches inside the circle).

6. Single flying change, both leads.

7. Canter serpentine with flying changes of lead, followed by a canter serpentine without changing leads (both hands).

8. Halt ("parade") from a trot.

9. Counter change of hand at a trot, in a half pass.

10. Half pass on a circle (haunches inside the circle) at a trot.

11. Full side-pass (75 degrees) along the short side, depart into trot straight forward, a few strides of extended trot.

12. Rein-back - extended trot.

(*) A bonus will be given to the rider who will present his horse in a passage, on the occasion of any one of these tests. The movement is not included in the test.

Third (or Master) Level (*)

Test 1

Enter (or open the gate, see text above).

Salute, reins completely dropped on the neck.

1. Piaffe.

2. Passage.

3. Canter pirouette.

4. Halt from canter (parade).

5. Canter - halt - rein back - canter - halt - rein back - canter, etc...

6. Passade: extended canter - slow down in three strides - half pirouette - extended canter, etc...

7. Passade: extended canter - slow down in three strides - half volte keeping the haunches inside - extended canter, etc...

8. Piaffe - collected canter.

9. Canter flying changes of lead every four strides on a circle.

10. Extended trot, halt in a few strides.

11. Extended canter - halt in three strides.

12. Extended canter - slow down in three strides - pirouette.

Test 2

Enter (or open the gate, see text above).

Salute, reins completely dropped on the neck.

1. Canter flying changes every three strides.

2. Canter flying changes every other stride.

3. At a canter: half pass - half pirouette - half pass - half pirouette, etc...

4. Canter pirouette - flying change straight forward.

5. Canter flying changes every three strides on a circle.

6. Canter flying changes every other stride on a circle.

7. Passage on a circle.

8. Passage on a figure eight.

9. Passage - extended trot.

10. Piaffe - passage - piaffe.

11. Collected canter - passage.

12. Counter changes of hand at a canter.

Test 3

Enter (or open the gate, see text above).

Salute, reins completely droppedd on the neck.

1. Canter tempi flying changes.

2. Canter pirouette to the right, followed by canter pirouette to the left.

3. Canter tempi flying changes, follow by canter flying changes every other stride.

4. Canter tempi flying changes on a circle.

5. The "gamut" (seven strides of canter, flying change, six strides, flying change, etc…two strides, flying change, one stride, flying change, two strides, flying change, three strides, etc…).

6. Passage on two tracks.

7. Pirouette at a piaffe.

8. Canter half pass on a circle, haunches outside (counter-canter).

9. Canter reversed pirouette.

10. La Guérinière's "square" at a canter.

11. Canter in place, or slightly forward (possibly "mézair").

12. Halt - canter pirouette.

(*) On the occasion of any one of these tests, a bonus will be given to the rider who performs a canter "parade" with the reins on the horse's neck. Likewise, a bonus will be given to the rider who performs a canter flying change on the straight, reins dropped on the horse's neck, without alteration of the gait.

Appendix 5

Description of movements

First Level, Test 1

1 to 3 - No comment.

4 - Extended free walk should be as impulsed as possible. Reins are adjusted as soon as the canter starts. Do not mistake extended walk, in which the horse remains collected although the action increases, with extended free walk, in which the horse is left to his natural balance, more or less on the shoulders, however with a minimal contact with the reins (let the reins slide).

5 - No comment.

6 - "Counted walk" is as slowed down a walk as possible, without any leg action from the rider (the legs are used only to start or restart the movement); it is characterized by a noticeable elevation of the withers, a diagonalization of the walk, an increased lightness in the contact, and a beginning of flexion of the hocks.

7 to 8 - No comment.

.
9 - For the transition trot-walk, it is advisable to use the right hand when the right front foot hits the ground and the left hand when the left front foot hits the ground.

10 to 11 - No comment..

12 - To get the lateral bending: inside hand in the position of indirect rein, weight (pelvis) inside.

First Level, Test 2

1 - No comment

2 - Four track shoulder-in, cf. **Ecole de Cavalerie**, Chapter 11.

3 - idem. Shoulder-in may be performed far from the wall. Here, the diagonal represents the wall of the arena.

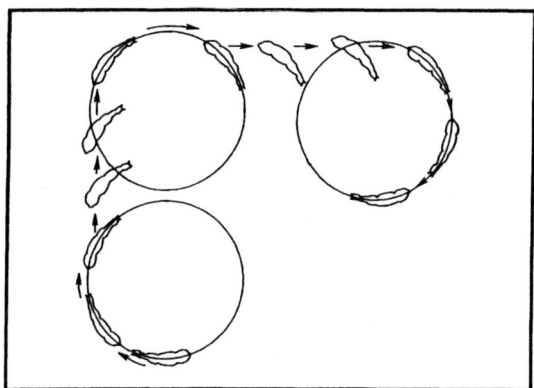

Fig. 31 - Circle - shoulder-in - circle.

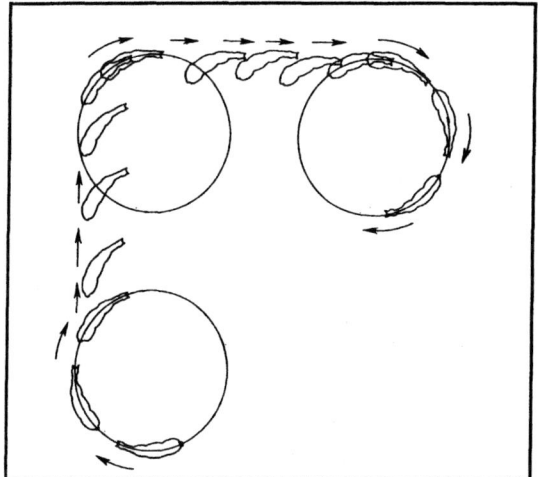

Fig. 32 - Circle - shoulder-in - circle - haunches-in - circle.

4 - Left shoulder-in on a circle to the right, and vice versa.

5 - idem.

6 - Turning to the right, left bend, and vice versa. The outside (with respect to the bend) hind leg acts as a pivot.

7 - Turning to the left, bend to the left, turning to the right, bend to the right. The outside (with respect to the bend) front leg acts as a pivot.

8 - For the definition of the "counted walk," see Test 1, exercise 6.

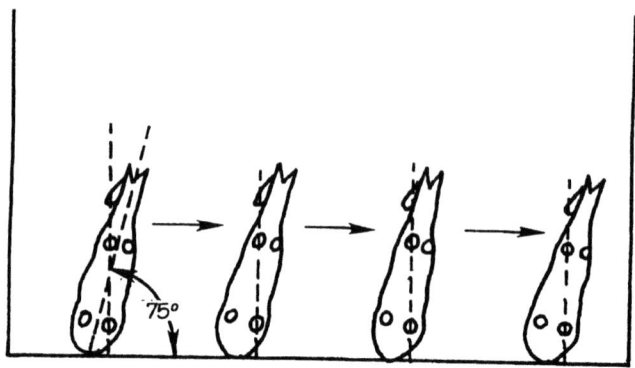

Fig. 33 - Full side-step to the right.

9 - idem.

10 - No comment.

11 - To perform in the length of the arena.

12 - No comment.

First Level, Test 3

1 - The exercise is described in chapter XI of "Ecole de Cavalerie" (Fig. 31).

2 - cf. Fig. 32.

3 - cf. Fig .33.

4 - In the half turn around the haunches, the bend is opposite to the direction of turning; in the reversed pirouette, on the contrary, the bend is direct. To perform on a straight line, for instance, the middle line, or the diagonal (Fig. 34).

5 to 9 - No comment.

10 - Canter depart straight ahead, at the end of the rotating movement.

11 - idem.

12 - No comment.

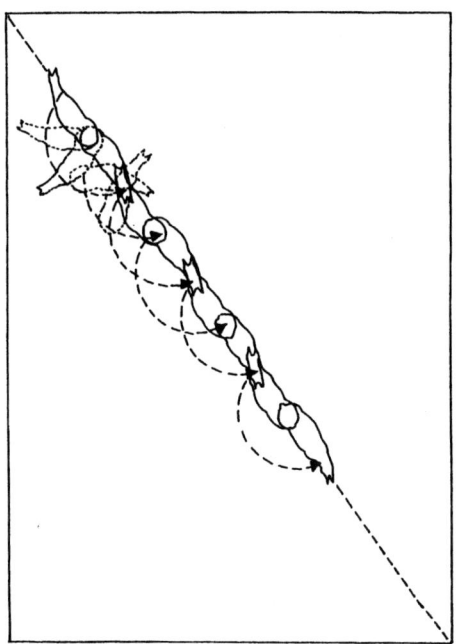

Fig. 34 - The waltz, right rein.
Horse keeps his right bend. Left hind foot and left
front foot alternatively used as pivots, as horse
turns around haunches, then around shoulders.

Second Level, Test 1

1 and 2 - No comment.

3 - For the means to use for the lateral bending, see First Level, Test 1, exercise 12.

4 and 5 - No comment.

6 - 15 meter circle.

7and 8 - On the diagonal.

9 and 10 - No comment.

11 - Slight inside "pli" (counter bending) in the side steps.

12 - No comment.

[133]

Second level, Test 2

1 - On the line AC, facing the judge.

2 - On the track.

3 - On the diagonal.

4 - No comment.

5 - 15 meter circle.

6 - Flying changes on a straight line, on X.

7 - No comment.

8 - On X.

9 - From left to right, then right to left.

10 - 15 meter circle.

11 and 12 - No comment.

Third Level, Test 1

1 to 8 - No comment.

9 - 15 meter circle.

10 to 12 - No comment.

Third Level, Test 2

1 to 3 - On the diagonal.

4 - Middle line.

5 - 15 meter circle.

6 - idem.

7 - idem.

8 - Figure eight in the width of the arena.

9 - On the diagonal.

10 and 11 - No comment..

12 - Four, cf. GP.

Third Level, Test 3

1 - On the diagonal.

2 - Anywhere inside the arena.

3 - On the diagonal.

4 - 15 meter circle.

5 - Itinerary ad libitum.

6 - On the diagonal, both hands.

7 - On X, both hands.

8 - 15 meter circle.

9 - On X.

10 - In the center of the arena; the sides of the square parallel to the sides of the arena, four strides at least of lateral canter.

11 - Line AC.

12 - Facing the judge.

Appendix 6

Evaluation Landmarks

If your horse behaves in this way	look for
Constantly changes leads from behind	S1, L6, L5
Bucks at a canter, and only at a canter	L6, C1
Walks and trots "crab-like"	L1 (*), T1
Walks and trots with one hind leg, and only one, "coming in"	Sacroiliac on the other side (*)
Is reluctant to canter on a given lead	T1
Lack of forward movement, abnormal sweat	T15 (*)
Violent and unexpected rebellion, more so when your weight comes forward	T3
Very narrow track of front feet	T3
Head high in a canter, rear end "hopping"	T3 (*)
Spooks, rears	C1 (*)
Very emotional	T1 (*), T3
Yawns, cribs (wind sucker)	T12 (*), T13 (*)
Does not raise his withers	C1 and then from T1 to T15
Navicular disease, lameness in front legs	C7 (*)
Front legs under his body	T1
Does not "reach" with front legs at a walk or trot	T1, T2, T3
Wrong relationship with the bit	C2 (*), C3 (*)
Shakes his head	C1, C2, C3, withers
Pulls out reins	withers(*)

(*) *Asterisk indicates that the information comes from Dr. Giniaux, either through his book* **What the Horses Have Told Me**, *or orally to* the author.

Important remarks:
1) Taking care of these levels does not prevent one from investigating and releasing all the compensations.
2) The author has limited himself in giving here all indications useful to the rider, or trainer, as concerns only the locomotion of the horse or his behavior. For all which concerns the pathology relating to vertebral blockings, read Dr. Giniaux's book. And call your veterinarian if needed.

French School books from XENOPHON PRESS

ANOTHER HORSEMANSHIP

Interested in the French tradition - *the riding in lightness?* Then this best selling book, written by Jean-Claude Racinet, the pre-eminent advocate of the French School of horsemanship in North America, best known for his clinics and articles in *DRESSAGE & CT*, as well as *RIDING IN LIGHTNESS* magazines, is for you.

This is a basic training manual, well illustrated, which will help you to understand and learn to ride *in lightness*.

ISBN 0-933316-03-8   *Perfect bound US$29.95 + US$3.00 P&H*

RACINET EXPLAINS BAUCHER

This book by Jean-Claude Racinet is a collection of essays in which the author discusses all aspects of the training methods of the 19th century French Master François Baucher. The author dispels many misconceptions about Baucher's methods, going in great detail about his *Second Method*.

This is absolutely necessary reading for any serious student of the riding in lightness, who has studied Jean-Claude Racinet's training manual **ANOTHER HORSEMAN-SHIP.**

ISBN 0-933316-08-9   *Perfect bound US$35.95 + US$3.00 P&H*

WHAT THE HORSES HAVE TOLD ME

The French equine veterinarian, Dr. Dominique Giniaux, knows that the first concern of any kind of medicine is to listen to the patient and one must know the questions to ask in order to determine accurately what troubles the patient is experiencing.

In the classical veterinary medicine, the dialogue is, unfortunately, indirect. Questions and answers are sometimes altered by the intermediaries. People in charge of the horse may misinterpret its behavior. Radiography gives not always the correct answer.

Upon becoming acquainted with human osteopathy, Dr. Giniaux taught himself to ask questions directly to the body of the equine patient without any other means than his hands. In this book, translated by Jean-Claude Racinet, Dr. Giniaux shares his experiences is an easy to understand language.

ISBN 0-933316-07-0   *Perfect bound US$29.95 + US$3.00 P&H*

HEALING HANDS

This book by Dr. Giniaux is about acupressure, that is to say, the art of alleviating your horse;s physical, and even sometimes mental, problems through applying pressure, with your thumb or index finger, on specific points of acupuncture.

Without interfering with your veterinarian, whose intervention remains necessary in most cases you will this way be able to check the course of a colic, or help your mare foaling; you will help your horse overcome a heat stroke, a crisis of emphysema,a hemorrhage, a bout of *tying-up, etc.*

ISBN 0-933316-12-7   *Perfect bound US$32.95 + US$3.00 P&H*

DRESSAGE IN THE FOURTH DIMENSION

Dr. Sherry L. Ackerman writes about the art, as opposed to the *sport,* of classical dressage. The author has positioned dressage in an integrated philosophical context, focusing on the principles of balance, harmony and lightness. Her work is concerned with liberating riders from the narrowly individualistic *I-nest.* She sees dressage as transformational, as an avenue to reflection, exploration, and self-knowledge, through which the rider may approach an experience of *non-duality.*

ISBN 0-933316-10-0   *Perfect bound US$25.95 + US$3.00 P&H*

Classics from Xenophon Press

ECOLE DE CAVALERIE

The 18th century French Master François de la Guèriniére wrote ECOLE DE CAVALERIE, universally considered to be the *bible* of classical horsemanship, frequently quoted, but seldom read.

This classical text comprises three parts, of which the second should be of utmost interest to every dressage trainer and rider, as it discusses in depth the training of the dressage horse.

We have published the pertinent chapters of the second part, including the original illustrations.

ISBN 0-933316-01-1   *Perfect bound US$34.95 + US$3.00 P&H*

THE GYMNASIUM OF THE HORSE

This is the first English translation of **DAS GYMNASIUM DES PFERDES,** the seminal work of the 19th century German Master Gustav Steinbrecht, who is credited with the laying of the foundation of German dressage riding.

"Today it stands a cornerstone of the equestrian literature, a work of truly remarkable coherence, comprehensiveness, and depth of understanding; its careful study cannot help but repay the thoughtful horseman many ways over," states 1968 Olympic Gold medalist William Steinkraus in his *Foreword* to **THE GYMNASIUM OF THE HORSE.**

ISBN 0-933316-04-6   *Perfect bound US$39.95 + US$3.00 P&H*

...and for any student of dressage

THE BASICS

This book, subtitled A Guideline For Successful Training, by Col. K. Albrecht von Ziegner, is a must for any dressage rider. The special importance of this book is the priority given the ten essential elements which the author believes necessary for the correct development of the horse, which he labels the *training tree.*

The author, a well known German clinician and teacher, who edited the 5th edition of Wilhelm Müseler's RIDING LOGIC, created THE BASICS as a useful complement to Müseler's book. Originally in English, it was translated in 1998 into German.

ISBN 0-933316-05-4   *Perfect bound US$27.95 + US$3.00 P&H*